# ITALY

# ITALY

*A Personal Anthology*

*by*

Bernard Wall

**NEWNES : LONDON**

Text set in Garamond

*Made and printed in Great Britain by*
*The Garden City Press Limited, Letchworth, Hertfordshire*
*for George Newnes Limited, Tower House*
*Southampton Street, London, W.C.2*

# CONTENTS

# CONTENTS

## INTRODUCTION

1964 is the fortieth anniversary of my first visit to Italy. Little did I think, when I was a small schoolboy, that my life would become so linked with Italians; that I would return not ten times to see the orange blossom shimmering in the sun, the terraces of vines in Tuscany, the ruins of the Roman Campagna, but nearer a hundred; and that I would have friends in almost every city from Turin to Palermo. But there it is.

Forty years ago Italy was different indeed from what it is today. From London it was a two days' journey by train and boat, with all the adventures of frontiers. There was the long night spent thundering across the back of France on what was then called the P.L.M.—the Paris-Lyons-Méditerranée—railway company. The dawn in Switzerland with the grey-uniformed Swiss customs officers making a polite gesture at the luggage, then steaming Swiss coffee while they changed the engine—with the exhilarating nip from the mountains turning pink in the sun. Then on and on to the Italian frontier: the warmth as one descended again into the plain, the blue of Lago Maggiore, the chirping of the crickets if the train stopped, the gentleness and warmth of the Italians who needed no excuse to begin a conversation. Then the stops in the stations with magic words written up in huge capitals—MILANO, BOLOGNA, FIRENZE, the scuttling of the Italian train through plains, across mountains (the Apennines) and down along the sea. Italian men always stand in the corridors talking, with their arms on the window bars looking out at the fields or the sea—the sea deep blue but sometimes patchy and slightly wrinkled, which only marks the windlessness of the Mediterranean compared with our northern oceans. In those days there were very few motorboats, but one would see fishing smacks, looking completely motionless, with brown lateen sails, and occasionally a steamer

7

in the distance plying between two big ports, Genoa, say, and Naples.

One's first arrival in Rome has always been a solemn moment. It was for the young provincials from Spain or even Britain, in the days of the Roman Empire; when they first experienced the bustle in the streets of the world's capital and greatest city. Medieval pilgrims broke into song or hymn at their long-awaited vision of the frame of the basilica, the shrine of St Peter; and eighteenth-century travellers were never tired of writing home, from their grand tour, about the earliest impact on them of the Colosseum and the Forum. Forty years ago life was in some ways more like that of the eighteenth century than that of our age of cosmonauts. One arrived at the little old peach-coloured station that was pulled down years ago. There was hardly any traffic in the streets except for the trams and the horse-carozzas. Rome was only half as big as it is now and one of the greatest pleasures of the inhabitants was meditative strolling in the streets, talking, and, of course, gesticulating. The Forum, before Mussolini's excavations, was a quiet wilderness with crickets and lizards. I remember chasing the lizards there, always foiled because they fled into the brick crannies of the ruins. And once I caught one. They tire very easily, the speed they rush about at is all show. I headed mine away from the brickwork into the rough grass, and kept it on the run. But there is no way of keeping a wild lizard in a hotel, so it was solemnly liberated again to sun itself where the poets and emperors had once strolled.

\* \* \* \* \* \*

Of course we always think things were better when we were young and artlessly in love. Then love turns into a sort of marriage. This is what has happened to me with regard to Italy over the years. With the marriage, the established and permanent relationship which is bound to go on, the love is still there, probably more solid, but it goes with knowledge and the spirit of criticism. There is also an element of something like boredom, at the sight of a group of Milanese business-men banqueting in a hotel, or an assembly of creased-trousered deputies of the majority party, or above all at the traffic that has flooded over all Italian cities, mostly thanks to Fiat who turn perhaps the world's best low-priced cars unendingly off their assembly lines in Turin. The magic of difference which made travel such an exciting experience

8

forty years ago has surely diminished. There is a sense in which Milanese business-men and Manchester business-men have become more alike—though nowadays the Milanese are perhaps more prosperous and go-ahead. The man driving a car has the same reactions and performs the same acts from Scotland to Sicily. Our increased alikeness is shown to the full in our airports —there is almost no difference between London airport and Rome's Fiumicino airport except in warmth and sunshine.

Italy is itself growing more uniform with the effects of the belated industrial revolution, or what some call Americanisation. But here there is still a long way to go. When you meet an Italian for the first time, the question you immediately ask him is: "What part of Italy are you from?" There is all the difference in the world between a manufacturer from rich Milan and a sinuous lawyer from poor Palermo. There are at least ten regions in Italy with quite distinct local dialects that are really languages in their own right, and despite the radio, the television and the cinema, which are imposing a uniform way of talking, the old ways persist.

Yet though Italy is one of the most "modern" countries, there is a continuity in the life of the people that has gone on for over two thousand years. One of my convictions is that the old Latin literature is still valid about many aspects of Italian life. Of course I am not thinking of an orator like Cicero who seems more like a pompous Victorian moraliser than like an Italian. But what about Catullus, with his passion for the faithless Lesbia, his desperate struggles to shake off the illness of jealousy, his almost (but never quite) suicidal frustration? I have come across more than one Catullus and more than one Lesbia, contemporaries in Milan or Rome. It is very difficult to explain this Italian temperament as regards affairs of the heart, as it is at once passionate, subtle (even Machiavellian) and naïf. English-speaking readers must adjust themselves to a quite new psychological climate as well as a physical one. Italians love the *present* much more, they are uninhibited and emotions are given free rein. Children are brought up like that. We have much to learn from them about how to enjoy life. And incidentally there are hardly any psychiatrists in Italy.

\* \* \* \* \* \*

When I was young I fell in love with the spiritual tradition of the Italian primitive painters. My love was for the undulating landscapes of Tuscany and Umbria, for places like Siena and Assisi. Here the spirit of St Francis still seems to live on in the little towns that crown the summits of the hills—and the terraced vines mounting upwards like steps to the medieval walls are absurdly familiar because we recognise the very scenes that, say, Fra Angelico used as background for a Crucifixion or a Resurrection. Even the people have familiar faces in Tuscany. Notice, if you go to Florence, how common it is to see people with refined, happy faces, but with noses slightly uptilted at the end with an air of alert curiosity—exactly like the goddesses Botticelli painted in his *Spring* or *Venus Rising From the Sea*.

This taste for primitive and spiritual Italy is natural enough. Later I developed another taste which is often disputed; anyway, it is an acquired taste. This is for the baroque.

I believe that you will never really understand Italy unless you understand the baroque. Whole towns are built in baroque architecture, Rome, for instance, or Lecce in the extreme south. Many people find the theatrical façades of the churches with statues writhing on top of them and the gorgeous glare of the interiors heavy, pompous or coarse. I agree my taste isn't spiritual. It isn't at the highest stage of artistic appreciation. But it is gay like the theatre or, better, the opera.

In fact all real italophiles love the opera, with its harmonious music and its melodramas, the lovesick heroes preparing to throw themselves over the cliff or to be shot at dawn. You do not object if the hero and the heroine both weigh twenty stone so long as they trill out their passions like birds in love and shriek their extravert despair. So, by baroque, I don't just mean architecture. Opera is baroque, because in it, too, passions are stretched out to the maximum of tension theatrically. The baroque is a way of life. The baroque situation, the lover starving to death, or wandering round with a revolver; the girl who is not quite sure whether to enter a convent or commit suicide—you can read about their melodrama every day in the newspapers in Italy. The grand baroque gesture, the gesture like that of the saints on St Peter's, who are tensed to the melodramatic limit. And then the lover does not quite starve to death; the girl does not take the veil after all. Tranquillity returns, as it does to the Mediterranean sea after sudden wild storms.

\* \* \* \* \* \*

Since I wrote the last paragraph I have just returned from one more visit to Italy—Rome again. I had not been there for a year, and it was forced on my thoughts that Italian life careers onwards so vertiginously that I would have to keep for ever on the run, mentally, to keep up with it. The journey from London Airport to Rome now takes two hours by jet plane. But the shock comes in Italy itself. One feels in all that shining and mechanical modernity that the Italians have now produced that one is entering and taking part in a new dynamic process. London by comparison seems static and Victorian. Italian cleanliness contrasts with English dirt. How the roles have been reversed since the war! For myself I preferred the slower world that existed everywhere in times gone by. I would not mind if the British were outstripped and dropped out of the world race, like the Spaniards. The Italians will surely be richer than the British in ten or fifteen years, if they continue as they are doing. May they keep that inner core of tranquillity and contemplation to which they return after all their storms; may their nerves keep padded; may they retain the sacrosanct habit of the siesta in the afternoons; may they find some solution to their urbanisation before it is too late; may they solve their parking problems; and may they remain happy.

B. W.

# Arrival

## *The Italian Miracle*

AT THE beginning of this year, light-heartedly but, as it happened, realistically, leading monetary experts from *The Financial Times* awarded a symbolic 1959 Oscar to the Italian lira on the grounds of its being a strong currency consolidated after many years of effort and reconstruction. On that occasion every Italian felt himself to have gained such recognition. The strength of a currency is the expression of a specific economic and political situation created by the endeavours of each citizen, from the lowliest worker to the agriculturalist, the manager, the industrialist and those who directly or indirectly bear the burden of government.

The award was followed by further spontaneous recognition of the progress of the Italian economy. It was, I think, British observers who coined the expression "The Italian Miracle" to describe Italy's reconstruction and subsequent economic expansion as a phenomenon, no less energetic in tempo or broad in scope than the German achievement. These impartial critics were not alone in their judgment, for foreign engineers, economists and industrialists alike have proved by their actions that they are increasingly interested in the Italian market. . . .

To foreigners the miracle lies in the fact that Italy has become a heavily industrialised country and that its products are successfully competing in markets in which they were hitherto unrepresented; that Italian industrialists are securing tenders for large-scale works outside Italy; that highly industrialised countries are buying Italian manufacturing

plant; and that Italian patented products are being manu-
factured under licence in Britain and America.

Italian exports extend to all sectors, from steel to chemical
equipment, from precision instruments to fertilisers;
plastics, man-made fibres and synthetic rubber. More than
80 per cent. of Italian exports consist of industrial products.
Export sales of Italian engineering products have made their
impact throughout world markets.

*The Financial Times,* January 16, 1961

I selected this piece by the sometime Italian finance minister,
Signor Pella, so that you will not get a shock when you arrive.
Be prepared for the miracle, then you can look around you at ease,
look into the past of Italy and have melancholy, poetic or joyful
thoughts, as you wish.

You may not want to go and visit the sprawling factories of
the great industrial towns, such as Milan, Turin and Brescia.
But wherever you go you will live with their products.

Truth to tell, I have only visited two Italian factories in my
life, but both are memorable. One is the Fiat works near Turin
which we were shown over by Professor Valletta who is the sort of
industrial planner Shaw might have idealised—a small vital man
with a mop of grey hair who talks about the works with a sort of
creative artistic affection. It takes hours, in a little bus, to travel
the whole route of the assembly lines from the initial stage in
which the rough metal is processed to the final achievement—
another Fiat car being driven away. The other factory I have
visited is the Olivetti assembly plant for typewriters near Pozzuoli:
an effort to bring work and money to the south of Italy. The great
Adriano Olivetti, who died in the 1950's, was one of the most
idealistic industrialists who ever existed. He founded a corpor-
ative organisation for management and workers, assisted the
workers in their syndical activities, led them in protest against
bad living conditions, provided better living conditions. Few
workers can have had a better life than those employed at
Pozzuoli, with a view over gardens to the Bay of Naples from
their assembly windows. . . .

But enough about factories for the time being. Italy can also
be seen as a place of joy and pleasure. I have drawn a good deal
on Byron in this book. I suppose he was a superficial, dilettante

kind of poet, like Ovid. Both of them were rich and lazy (though laziness in writing is much misunderstood—with a lazy attitude you may well write more books than a man would who is always worrying and tensed up).

One thing I like about Byron is that he didn't moralise too much about Italy. The British moralising attitude about Italian misrule helped the Italians to achieve their national unity. But it isn't this way that I have approached the sister country. Of course there is a more secret and trivial reason for quoting so much Byron, too. I read Byron in Italy. I will never forget the near ecstasy of a long Christmas season years ago before the war, spent at a little hotel at the top of the Spanish Steps in Rome (it has been rebuilt and only millionaires could go there now). The view of steel-blue sky over the panorama of the city from the window, the walks through crisp dry air in the Pincio gardens, the odd hour spent on one of those benches (there seemed to be no motor-cars then). And Byron under my arm on the walks.

### *Italy*

With all its sinful doings, I must say,
　　That Italy's a pleasant place to me,
Who love to see the Sun shine every day,
　　And vines (not nail'd to walls) from tree to tree
Festoon'd, much like the back scene of a play,
　　Or melodrama, which people flock to see,
When the first act is ended by a dance
In vineyards copied from the south of France.

I like on Autumn evenings to ride out,
　　Without being forced to bid my groom be sure
My cloak is round his middle strapp'd about,
　　Because the skies are not the most secure;
I know too that, if stopp'd upon my route,
　　Where the green alleys windingly allure,
Reeling with grapes red waggons choke the way,—
In England 'twould be dung, dust, or a dray.

I also like to dine on becaficas,
    To see the Sun set, sure he'll rise tomorrow,
Not through a misty morning twinkling weak as
    A drunken man's dead eye in maudlin sorrow,
But with all Heaven t' himself; the day will break as
    Beauteous as cloudless, nor be forced to borrow
That sort of farthing candlelight which glimmers
Where reeking London's smoky caldron simmers.

I love the language, that soft bastard Latin,
    Which melts like kisses from a female mouth,
And sounds as if it should be writ on satin,
    With syllables which breathe of the sweet South,
And gentle liquids gliding all so pat in,
    That not a single accent seems uncouth,
Like our harsh northern whistling, grunting guttural,
Which we're obliged to hiss, and spit, and sputter all.

I like the women too (forgive my folly),
    From the rich peasant cheek of ruddy bronze,
And large black eyes that flash on you a volley
    Of rays that say a thousand things at once,
To the high dama's brow, more melancholy,
    But clear, and with a wild and liquid glance,
Heart on her lips, and soul within her eyes,
Soft as her clime, and sunny as her skies.

Eve of the land which still is Paradise!
    Italian beauty! didst thou not inspire
Raphael, who died in thy embrace, and vies
    With all we know of Heaven, or can desire,
In what he hath bequeath'd us?—in what guise
    Though flashing from the fervour of the lyre,
Would *words* describe thy past and present glow,
While yet Canova can create below?

                    LORD BYRON "Italy and England"

*Milan: towards heaven or towards the future or towards what?*

*Piedmont produces soldiers, Fiat cars,
and some of the finest wines in Italy*

But neither the Median forests, that rich land, nor fair
    Ganges,
Nor Hermus rolling in gold
Compares with Italy—no, not Bactra nor the Indies
Nor all Arabia's acres of spice-enrichened soil.
This land of ours has never been ploughed by bulls fire-
    breathing
Nor sown with dragon's teeth;
It has never known a harvest of serried helmeted spearmen:
Rather is it a country fulfilled with heavy corn and
Campanian wine, possessed by olives and prosperous
    herds.
Here the charger gallops on to the plain in his pride,
Here the white-fleeced flocks and the bull, a princely victim
Washed over and over in Clitumnus' holy water,
Head our Roman triumphs to the temples of the gods.
Here is continual spring and a summer beyond her season;
Cattle bear twice yearly, apples a second crop.
No bloodthirsty tigers are found here, no fierce young lions
    roar,
No monkshood grows to deceive and poison the wretch who
    picks it,
Nor does the scaly snake slither at such great length
On the ground or gather himself into so many coils here.
Number our noble cities and all the works of our hands,
The towns piled up on toppling cliffs, the antique walls
And the rivers that glide below them.
Must I commemorate the Upper sea and the Lower?
The lakes so great? Lake Larius the greatest of them
    all,
Lake Benacus that tosses and growls like a little ocean?
Shall I mention our harbours, the mole that was built to
    bar the Lucrine
And made the deep cry out in mighty indignation
Where the sound of Julius murmurs with the sound of the
    sea locked out
And Tyrrhene tides flow through a canal into Averno?

17

Veins of silver and copper Italy too has revealed
And rivers running with gold.

*The Georgics of Virgil* (Book II)
Trans. C. DAY LEWIS

### *Arriving in Italy*

Those of us who had not fallen asleep glanced casually down at the Alps. They lay beneath our wings like a model in a geological museum, and though it was July, many a summit was still white.

There comes over me sometimes a sense of the wonder and fantasy of this age, and, as I adjusted my chair to a more comfortable angle, I thought how preposterous it was to be speeding through the sky to Rome, many of us unaware of the great barrier which awed and terrified our ancestors. While I looked down, trying in vain to identify the passes—the Mont Cenis, the St Gothard, the Great St Bernard and the Little, and the famous Brenner—a series of pictures flashed through my mind. . . . Hannibal and his hungry elephants, Charles the Bald dying in the Mont Cenis, the Emperor Henry IV hurrying through the blizzards of January, 1077, to make peace with the Pope, while the Empress and her ladies were strapped into ox-hides and let down over the frozen slopes like bundles of hay.

"Would you like a glucose sweet or a peppermint?" asked the air hostess, as we crossed the Alps.

The feelings of many centuries of Romeward bound travellers were expressed in a sentence by Lady Mary Wortley Montagu, when she wrote from Turin in 1720. "I am now, thank God, happily past the Alps." Even in her day, when the Grand Tour was beautifully organized, the passage of the Alps was full of danger or at least of apprehension. It was usual for the coaches to be unbolted and sent over on the backs of mules, while the travellers, wrapped in bearskins and wearing beaver caps and mittens, sat in armchairs slung between two poles and were carried over the pass by nimble mountaineers. Montaigne, who

18

went to Italy to forget his gallstones, was carried up the Mont Cenis, but on the summit was transferred to a toboggan: and in the same pass Horace Walpole's lapdog, Tory, was seized and eaten by a wolf. Even while these random thoughts passed through my mind, we had left the Alps far behind us, and it was not long before we were fastening our belts for Rome.

The drive from the airport into Rome was long and dreary, but all the time I was thinking with pleasure of the "room with balcony" to which I was speeding. For weeks I had lived with a mental picture of this balcony, though I had never seen it. There might not be bougainvillaea, I told myself, but no doubt there would be geraniums in pots; and I would stand there in the evening and watch the sun setting behind St Peter's, as so many had done before me, while the swifts—would there be swifts in July?—would cut the air with cries which every Roman child knows means "Gesù . . . Gesù . . . Gesù!"

H. V. MORTON *A Traveller in Rome*

The journeys made by earlier travellers to Italy were more exhausting than our own. But their pains were rewarded. They really *travelled*. Alice Meynell and Gibbon arrived in Italy from the north.

### The Watershed

Black mountains pricked with pointed pine
    A melancholy sky.
Out-distanced was the German vine,
    The sterile fields lay high.
From swarthy Alps I travelled forth
Aloft; it was the north, the north;
    Bound for the Noon was I.

I seemed to breast the streams that day;
    I met, opposed, withstood
The northward rivers on their way,
    My heart against the flood—

My heart that pressed to rise and reach
And felt the love of altering speech,
    Of frontiers, in its blood.

But oh, the unfolding South! the burst
    Of summer! Oh to see
Of all the southward brooks the first!
    The travelling heart went free
With endless streams; that strife was stopped;
And down a thousand vales I dropped,
    I flowed to Italy.

ALICE MEYNELL


    I climbed Mount Cenis, and descended into the plain of
Piedmont, not on the back of an elephant,* but on a light
osier seat, in the hands of the dexterous and intrepid
chairman of the Alps.

EDWARD GIBBON Autobiography


    It is not always easy to bring before our minds other, more
sorrowful aspects of Italy. Yet half of all Italian poetry and
English poetry about Italy has stressed the woes of the country.
You must remember how, from the fall of the Roman Empire
in the fourth century A.D. until just under a hundred years ago,
the Italians were never free from invasions—of the French,
Spaniards, Germans and Saracens. The country was divided up
into little states often carved out by foreigners and under foreign
rule. Both foreigners and Italians believed that a great decadence
had befallen Italy—and this feeling was nearly always enhanced,
as we shall see, by memories of the grandeur of Imperial Rome.

Italia! oh Italia! thou who hast
The fatal gift of beauty, which became
A funeral dower of present woes and past,
On thy sweet brow is sorrow plough'd by shame,
And annals graved in characters of flame.

*A reference to Hannibal's entry into Italy.

Oh, God! that thou wert in thy nakedness
Less lovely or more powerful, and couldst claim
Thy right, and awe the robbers back, who press
To shed thy blood, and drink the tears of thy distress;

Then might'st thou more appal; or, less desired,
Be homely and be peaceful, undeplored
For thy destructive charms; then, still untired,
Would not be seen the armed torrents pour'd
Down the deep Alps; nor would the hostile horde
Of many-nation'd spoilers from the Po
Quaff blood and water; nor the stranger's sword
Be thy sad weapon of defence, and so,
Victor or vanquish'd, thou the slave of friend or foe.

LORD BYRON *Childe Harold's Pilgrimage*

# Milan and Lombardy

ITALIANS LOVE to describe cities as "beautiful." *"Venezia è una bella città. Firenze è una bella città."* But no one could say *"Milano è una bella città."* It has other qualities; but no, Milan is not beautiful.

I think of it first as a mixture of Vienna and Manchester. The late café life, the emphasis on pleasure, the restaurants under vines, the music bursting from doorways open on to a piazza, the crowds meeting their friends at the opera—all these things remind me of Vienna as it used to be. There is something Viennese, too, about the electric trams that hiss along the streets packed with business-men carrying brief-cases; though the conductor, who sits up on a special guichet by the electric doors, as on a throne, is specially Italian.

But who wants to keep to the main streets and the public conveyances all the time? Further afield there are dark and narrow streets, blind factory walls and gloomy canals. In the yards we see those heaps of scrap iron, refuse of any industrial city. Workmen troop to clock in for their shift at the machines. This is Manchester.

The Mancunian aspect of Milan developed only in the last century with the growth of the mills and of heavy industry, and with a culture that has extended over two millennia. In the latter days of the Roman Empire, when St Augustine visited it as he describes in his *Confessions*, it was already the leading city of the north, more honest, more laborious, than Rome; guided by the genius of Ambrose—Sant' Ambrogio. When the Nordic barbarians broke into the garden of Lombardy for the first time the

22

disaster they brought with them lasted only for a while. Little by little the old Celtic-Roman civilisation softened their manners and assimilated them. In the Middle Ages the Milanese developed commerce. Their society, like that of many other cities of Northern and Central Italy, was a middle-class and trading one. The city became a Free Commune and the citizens struggled bitterly against the feudalism of the Holy Roman Empire. Northern Italian history is more like that of ancient Greece than that of France or England. The Free Communes corresponded in some measure to the Greek "Democracies". They failed for similar reasons of internal strife and external pressure. The type of government that succeeded the Free Communes, which consisted in the ascendency of a family usually called a Signoria or Signory, in some ways resembled a Greek "Tyranny". The "tyrants" or "overlords" were often brilliant, but they were nearly always baleful. Milan endured two successive dynasties of them—the Visconti and the Sforza. The latter shepherded the city into the golden age of the Renaissance.

\* \* \* \* \* \*

After the fall of the Sforza the city was ruled by foreigners. First came the French, then the Spaniards, then the Austrians. The French ousted the Austrians during the Napoleonic wars and the Milanese enjoyed a period of intellectual ferment and political liberalism. The city was made the capital first of the Cisalpine Republic, then of the Napoleonic Kingdom of Italy. This French interlude had a decisive effect on modern Italian history. To the intelligentsia, who had experienced a foretaste of national unity under the French hegemony, the return of the Austrians after the fall of Napoleon, and the imposition of the principles of the Holy Alliance, seemed an intolerable set-back. Poets wrote bitterly and satirically against their Germanic rulers, and the Milanese carried on a cold war—with occasional warm interludes—against the Hapsburgs until

23

1859. In that year Lombardy was united with Piedmont. Perhaps the most striking thing about Milan in the second half of the nineteenth century was the enormous growth of population. Before the First World War there were some 600,000 inhabitants. The population today numbers over one and a half millions. In size it is the second city of Italy.

BERNARD WALL *Italian Art, Life and Landscape*

Here is a description of daily life in Milan by Aubrey Menen, the novelist, who now lives in Rome. He is one of the best psychological writers about the Italian character today.

## *The Milanese*

It was twelve-thirty on a sunlit day in March. We were in the heart of the city, and all Milan was trotting rapidly to luncheon. We left the car and we trotted, too—my Milanese friend, who was busy making a fortune in machine tools, and I, who had come to Milan to see one of the most famous sights of Italy—the new prosperity which has come to parts of the country in the last five years.

We trotted into a bar. My friend rapped out an order for two aperitifs. The barman flickered his hands among the bottles and glasses. Within ten seconds the aperitifs had been served: within thirty we had drunk them. We trotted to the door, we regained the car. My friend snatched an illegal parking ticket from the windscreen, leapt into the driving seat and flung the car into motion. He was enjoying himself. He was showing off the pace of living in the thriving, prosperous, bustling city of Milan.

It is true that we spent the next twenty minutes crawling round the streets at two miles an hour, looking for a parking place. But my friend upheld the honour of Milan by talking twice as fast as usual.

"Making so much money," he said, biting off his words, "all of us. That's the trouble. Make money. . . ."(Everybody in Milan makes money.) ". . . Buy cars. . . ." (Every-

24

body in Milan seems to have a car.) ". . . Can't park them.
. . ." (Everybody in Milan seems to be going somewhere
always.) ". . . We'll have to tear down the city to park the
cars we buy with all the money we can't stop making. Blast
that man: nipped in before me. Nobody would mind if we
do. Leave the Duomo, La Scala. Tear down all *this*," he
said, waving a rapid hand at a row of seventeenth-century
façades. "No good, anyway. Provincial stuff. Skyscrapers
instead. Wha'-d'you think of our skyscrapers?"

I do not repeat his actual words. Such sentences as I have
written cannot be spoken in Italian even by the swift-
tongued Milanese. Grammar forbids it. But I attempt to
convey the clipped, rattling way they talk, like an errand
boy running a stick across iron railings. It is very stimu-
lating, if and when you can make out what they are
saying.

As for the skyscrapers, that was an easy question to
answer. In every city of the world, the inhabitants always
prefer the latest skyscraper that has been run up to any of
the others. So I said, "The Pirelli is fine."

"Isn't it? Gleaming, eh? Sleek. Funny thing—*these*
people . . ." and out went his hand towards the façades of
the seventeenth-century palaces that prevented him parking
his car, "*they* wanted to hide the fact they were rolling in
money." The façades were, indeed, unpretentious affairs of
no more than three low stories. "Now today," he said,
"we boast about it. Look at the Pirelli, Shouts money at
you. Old man's dead now, old man Pirelli. But he did the
right thing. *Shouts* money," he said, savouring his own
phrase. "We like that in Milan. We like money. But we're
not vulgar. Not at all. Are we? Eh?"

"No, no, no, not at all," I said firmly. I have no objection to vulgarity and, after all, was he not taking me to
luncheon?

"Why?" he said. "Ask you, why? Tell you. We don't
like money as money. Like spending it. In handfuls. Hat-
fuls. Left, right, centre. Spend. Spend money, got to make
it, eh? At least we say so. Italians elsewhere are not so sure.
Spend money, yes. Make it? Well, not today. Tomorrow,

maybe. Or perhaps it will fall from the blue skies of beautiful Italy. But we Milanese . . . no . . . work, make it, spend it. Throw it away on the rest of our lazy countrymen. Ahhh!" he said. The car jumped as though it had been kicked, and we were parked.

The car doors were slammed, and we trotted through the narrow streets of the old city, past the modest stucco façade of the Scala Opera House, past the huge pile of the famous cathedral of Milan with its ugly muddle of Renaissance and Gothic, and came to our restaurant. Still at an ostrich pace, we entered, sat, and were instantly engulfed in waiters and bills of fare that seemed as vast as the sails of a ship.

AUBREY MENEN
*Speaking the Language Like a Native*

But the master of all foreign writers in the art of probing the Italian character was a Frenchman—Stendhal. He is also one of the greatest of all novelists. We shall be quoting him a lot, from his magnificent memoirs of Italian life as he lived it at the beginning of the nineteenth century, and from his great Italianate novel *The Charterhouse of Parma*. Stendhal admired the Italians for their passions, their spontaneity, their vitality, and was never tired of contrasting these characteristics with the frigid reflectiveness of his fellow-countrymen. Of all Italian cities, Stendhal loved Milan most. This was partly because of the Opera—the Scala—which was the greatest centre of social life in the whole country, but also because it was the city he knew as a young officer in Napoleon's armies. Also he had a beautiful mistress in Milan.

## Love Story in Milan

There is nothing rarer, here in Milan, than to fall in with an Italian eager to embark upon a narrative with none for audience but another of his own sex. The effort is usually reserved for the company of some more tender feminine acquaintance, or at best, for an occasion when the narrator is well established in the reassuring luxury of a *poltrona*

26

(easy-chair). The tale my new friend told me was enriched with a wealth of picturesque circumstance, more often than not described in gesture; I pass it on in an abridged version.

"Some sixteen years since, a man of great estate, by name Zilietti, a banker from Milan, arrived one evening in Brescia. His first act was to visit the theatre; and there, in a box, his attention was captured by the striking features and the extreme youth of an unknown woman. Now Zilietti was forty years old, and had recently been amassing wealth to the tune of millions; indeed, one might have suspected that he had no care in all the world save money. Moreover, his journey to Brescia concerned some business matter, whose successful issue depended upon a prompt return to Milan. In an instant, every thought of money had flown from his head. With some difficulty, he managed to find an instant to whisper a word or two in the young enchantress' ear. You know her, of course: her name is Gina, and she was the wife of a man of noble birth and high fortune. In the end, Zilietti succeeded in persuading her to elope with him. And for sixteen years now he has adored her; yet, for that her husband is still alive, he has never been able to make her his wife.

"Six months ago, Gina's lover fell ill—for you must know that for some two years now, she has taken herself a lover, the poet Malaspina—that excessively handsome fellow whom you met recently in the *salon* of la Bibin Catena. Zilietti, whose love is not a whit diminished since that first encounter, was desperately jealous. Every instant of his time which was not spent among his lodgers was passed with Gina. She meanwhile, distracted with the knowledge that her lover lay in danger of his life, yet well aware that every servant about her person was salaried with gold to spy and straightway report upon her every step, ordered her coachman to set her down by the Cathedral porch; and thence, making her way secretly through the crypts and passages beneath the nave, she emerged upon the further side, where the Archbishop has his residence, found the shop of an old-clothes-merchant, and equipped

27

herself with male attire and a set of ropes. Not knowing how else to reach home safely with her purchases, she bundled the garments out of sight beneath the folds of her own dress, and regained her carriage without further incident. No sooner was she inside her own front door than she asserted that she felt unwell, and locked herself alone in the privacy of her bedroom. At the first hour after midnight, having knotted her ropes into the rough semblance of a ladder, she fastened one end of it to her balcony and clambered silently down into the street. Her apartment, incidentally, was a *piano nobile* (first floor) at some considerable distance from the ground. At half past one in the morning, disguised as a man, she reached her lover's bedside. Malaspina was in the seventh heaven of delight; if he had felt sorrow at the oncoming of death, it was only because he had despaired of a last glimpse of his beloved. 'Yet come no more, sweet Gina,' said he, when at length, towards three in the morning, she found the courage to tear herself from his side. 'The doorkeeper of this house is in the pay and service of Zilietti; I am poor, nor are you richer than I am; yet wealth and luxury are woven into the pattern of your life, and I should die in despair if I should know myself the occasion of a rift between yourself and Zilietti.'

"Gina tore herself out of his arms. Yet at two o'clock in the morning of the day following, there came a tapping at the window of Malaspina's apartment, which, like Gina's, was situated on the first floor, and looked out upon one of those great stone balconies which are so frequent in Italy. It was Gina, who, having climbed out of her own window with the aid of a rope-ladder, had then hoisted herself up to that of her lover by the same means. Yet when she found him, he was lost in a delirium, and could say no word but her name, nor speak of anything, save of his passion for her. And for thirteen nights without respite the same expedition took place, until at length Malaspina was well out of danger."

STENDHAL *Rome, Naples and Florence*

Most people don't like the Cathedral of Milan, which is enormous, late Gothic, and covered with pinnacles that make me think of a porcupine. The real historical heart of Milan is in the Scala opera house, just round the corner, where you may hear Maria Callas sing. The Scala is still a social centre and the Milanese still meet their friends in the foyer. The spiritual centre of Milan is the church of St Ambrose, the patron saint of the city. Parts of the church date back to St Ambrose's own period: the fourth century. The patron saint himself is buried in the crypt.

This is how St Augustine, a contemporary, wrote of St Ambrose.

## Ambrose in Milan

But although my mind was full of questions and I was restless to argue out my problems, I did not pour out my sorrows to you, praying for your help. I even thought of Ambrose simply as a man who was fortunate, as the world appraises fortune, because he was held in such high esteem by such important people. His celibacy seemed to me the only hardship which he had to bear. As for his secret hopes, his struggles against the temptations which must come to one so highly placed, the consolations he found in adversity, and the joy he knew in the depths of his heart when he fed upon your Bread, these were quite beyond my surmise for they lay outside my experience. For his part he did not know how I was tormented or how deeply I was engulfed in danger. I could not ask him the questions I wished to ask in the way that I wished to ask them, because so many people used to keep him busy with their problems that I was prevented from talking to him face to face. When he was not with them, which was never for very long at a time, he was reviving his body with the food that it needed or refreshing his mind with reading. When he read, his eyes scanned the page and his heart explored the meaning, but his voice was silent and his tongue was still. All could approach him freely and it was not usual for visitors to be announced, so that often, when we came to see him, we found him reading like this in silence, for he never read aloud. We would sit there quietly, for no one had the heart to disturb him when he was so engrossed in study. After a time we went away again, guessing that in the short time when he was free from the turmoil of other men's affairs and was able to refresh his own mind, he would not wish to be distracted. Perhaps he was afraid that, if he read aloud, some obscure passage in the author he was reading might raise a question in the mind of an attentive listener, and he would then have to explain the meaning or even discuss some of the more difficult points. If he spent his time in this way, he would not manage to read as much as he wished. Perhaps a more likely reason why he read to himself was that he needed to spare his voice, which quite easily became hoarse. But whatever his reason, we may be sure it was a good one.

## *Singing in Milan*

It was not long before this that the Church at Milan had begun to seek comfort and spiritual strength in the practice of singing hymns, in which the faithful united fervently with heart and voice. It was only a year, or not much more, since Justina, the mother of the boy emperor Valentinian, had been persecuting your devoted servant Ambrose in the interests of the heresy into which the Arians had seduced her. In those days your faithful people used to keep watch in the church, ready to die with their bishop, your servant. My mother, your handmaid, was there with them, taking a leading part in that anxious time of vigilance and living a life of constant prayer. Although I was not yet fired by the warmth of your Spirit, these were stirring times for me as well, for the city was in a state of alarm and excitement. It was then that the practice of singing hymns and psalms was introduced, in keeping with the usage of the Eastern churches, to revive the flagging spirits of the people during their long and cheerless watch. Ever since then the custom has been retained, and the example of Milan has been followed in many other places, in fact in almost every church throughout the world.

SAINT AUGUSTINE *Confessions*

Probably Milan's most famous art treasure is the Last Supper at Santa Maria della Grazie. It is faded and disappointing.


## *Leonardo and the Last Supper*

When Ludofico Sforza became duke of Milan in 1493, he invited Leonardo most ceremoniously to come and play the lute before him. Leonardo took an instrument he had himself constructed of silver in the shape of a horse's head, a form calculated to render the tone louder and more sonorous. Leonardo was one of the best *improvisatori* in verse of his time. He surpassed all the musicians who had assembled to perform and so charmed the duke by his varied gifts that the nobleman delighted beyond measure in his society. The duke prevailed on him to paint a Nativity for an altarpiece to be sent as a present to the Emperor (Maximilian I). For the Dominican monks of Santa Maria della Grazie at Milan, Leonardo painted the *Last Supper*. This is a most beautiful and admirable work. The master gave so much beauty and majesty to the heads of the Apostles that he was constrained to leave the Christ unfinished, convinced as he was that he could not render the divinity of the Redeemer. Even so, this work has always been held in the highest estimation by the Milanese and by foreigners as well. Leonardo rendered to perfection the doubts and anxieties of the Apostles, their desire to know by whom their Master is to be betrayed. All their faces show their love, terror, anger, grief, or bewilderment, unable as they are to fathom the meaning of the Lord. The spectator is also struck by the determination, hatred, and treachery of Judas. The whole is executed with the most minute exactitude. The texture of the tablecloth seems actually made of linen.

The story goes that the prior was in a great hurry to see the picture done. He could not understand why Leonardo should sometimes remain before his work half a day together, absorbed in thought. He would have him work away, as he compelled the labourers to do who were digging in his garden, and never put the pencil down. Not content with seeking to hurry Leonardo, the prior even complained to the duke, and tormented him so much that at length he sent for Leonardo and courteously entreated him to finish the work. Leonardo, knowing the duke to be an intelligent man, explained himself as he had never bothered to do to the prior. He made it clear that men of genius are sometimes producing most when they seem least to labour, for their minds are then occupied in the shaping of those conceptions to which they afterwards give form. He told the duke that two heads were yet to be done: that of the Saviour, the likeness of which he could not hope to find on earth and had not yet been able to create in his imagination in perfection of celestial grace; and the other, of Judas. He said he wanted to find features fit to render the appearance of a man so depraved as to betray his benefactor, his Lord, and the Creator of the world. He said he would still search but as a last resort he could always use the head of that troublesome and impertinent prior. This made the duke laugh with all his heart. The prior was utterly confounded and went away to speed the digging in his garden. Leonardo was left in peace.

VASARI Lives of the Painters

The country round Milan is flat and rather boring. But in compensation the Milanese have their lake district within little over an hour's distance by car.

I cannot resist including this passage about Lake Como by the most famous of all Milanese writers, Alessandro Manzoni. It is taken from *The Betrothed,* Italy's greatest novel, a book that mirrors the Italians to themselves and others, as Don Quixote does for Spaniards. It is a story of poor peasants and rich oppressors, deeply Christian in spirit and full of gentle irony.

### Lake Como

Very quietly they made their way to the spot on the lakeside to which they had been directed. They found the boat

*The Fiat works near Turin turns out 4,000 cars a day*

"That branch of the Lake of Como . . ." We see where Italy
and Switzerland meet in the shape of the villa roof below us

ready, exchanged the password, and went aboard. The boatman punted the boat away from the bank with one oar, then took up the other and rowed out with both arms into the open lake towards the opposite shore. There was not a breath of wind; the lake lay flat and smooth, and would have seemed quite motionless but for the gentle, tremulous swaying of the moon, reflected from high up in the sky. The only sounds were the slow, sluggish lapping of the waves on the pebbly shore, farther away the gurgle of water swishing around the piles of the bridge, and then the measured splash of those two oars as they cut the blue surface of the lake, suddenly came out dripping, and then plunged in once again. The wash of the boat, joining up behind the stern, left a rippling furrow which drew farther and farther away from the shore.

\* \* \* \* \* \*

Farewell, mountains springing from the waters and rising to the sky; rugged peaks, familiar to any man who has grown up in your midst, and impressed upon his mind as clearly as the features of his nearest and dearest; torrents whose varying tones he can pick out as easily as the voices of his family; villages scattered white over the slopes, like herds of grazing sheep; farewell! How sadly steps he who was reared among you, as he draws away! At that moment, in the mind even of him who leaves you of his own accord, lured by the hope of finding fortune elsewhere, the dreams of riches lose their charm; he finds himself wondering how he could ever have resolved to leave you, and would turn back even then, but for the hope of one day returning rich. The more he advances into the plain, the more his eye flinches away in weariness and disgust from its vast uniformity; the air seems lifeless and heavy; gloomily and listlessly he enters the bustling cities; the houses heaped on houses, the streets leading to more streets, seem to prevent him breathing there; and as he stands before the building which foreigners admire, he thinks with restless longing of a little acre in his own village, of a cottage which he has long marked for his own and will buy when he returns wealthy to his native mountains.

But what of one who has never even cast a passing wish beyond those mountains, who had set all the plans of her future among them, and is then driven far away from them by a perverse power! What of one who, suddenly torn from her dearest habits and thwarted in her dearest hopes, leaves those mountains to go and seek out strangers whom she has never wished to know, and can look forward to no definite time for her return! Farewell home where, sitting among her secret thoughts, she had learned to pick out from all others the sound of a footstep awaited with a mysterious awe. Farewell house that was still not hers; house at which she had so often glanced hastily in passing, not without a blush; house in which the imagination had pictured a perpetual calm, unending life of married bliss. Farewell church, wherein her soul had so often found serenity in singing the praises of the Lord; where a ritual had already been prepared by a promise: where the secret longing of her heart was to be solemnly blessed, and love ordained and called holy: farewell! He who gave you so much happiness is everywhere, and never disturbs the joy of His children, except to prepare for them another greater and more certain.

ALESSANDRO MANZONI *The Betrothed*
Trans. ARCHIBALD COLQUHOUN

But this beautiful lakeland region has also had its horrors. In April 1945 I was in Rome with the Allies. We had spent the whole winter freezing in requisitioned lodgings in the new quarters beyond Porta Pinciana. The war was dragging on and on, then suddenly there was an allied leap forward, the German armies collapsed, the big industrial cities of Northern Italy were in revolt, and Mussolini, so the news came to us, had been captured and killed by Italian partisans. That evening as a few of the details filtered through to us I was with an Italian poet, the late Umberto Saba. He said to me that Mussolini and his mistress, with other Fascists, had been hung from meat-hooks in Piazzale

Loreto in Milan, for this is what we had heard at the time. The atmosphere was tense amongst all of us. It would be hard to explain in a few words the impression made on Italians and on those of us who had lived in Italy under Mussolini's regime, at the disappearance of the dictator. His face and gestures were familiar to all through a million reproductions. Many of us had heard him addressing the Fascist crowds from his balcony in Palazzo Venezia. Though only a moderate tyrant in comparison with Hitler, he had been a disturbing father-figure, or a kind of ambiguous god, whose Eye was supposed to have watched everything and everybody. Saba said, thinking of the meat-hook: "Do you notice how everybody is giving an uneasy look at the meat on their plates."

This is what really happened.

## The Death of Mussolini

At dawn on April 27 [1945] Mussolini and a few other Italians—among them Claretta Petacci, who had reached Menaggio—joined a German motorised column retreating to the north. They left Menaggio and had driven little more than ten miles when they discovered that the road, narrow at that point and squeezed between a wall of rock and the lake, had been blocked with a felled tree and a head of stones. As the whole column came to a halt, a few partisans appeared. After several hours, during which the German commanding officer was taken for negotiations to partisan headquarters miles away, the Germans obtained permission to proceed on the condition that they took no Italians along. They were warned that all vehicles would be inspected on their passage through Dongo, a village a few miles farther on.

While the other Italians were compelled to stay behind and were taken prisoner by the partisans, Mussolini went on with the Germans: he wore one of their topcoats as a disguise. At about 3 o'clock p.m., in Dongo, the inspection of the German column began. Mussolini sat hunched in his German coat, with hat pulled down to hide his face, pretending to sleep. But on the second round of inspection he was recognised and taken prisoner by a small group of partisans. He did not struggle or offer resistance of any sort. One of the captors, a certain "Bill"—all partisans assumed fictitious first names and used no other—later wrote: "His glance is absent . . . his face waxy . . . his beard makes his chin look darker and increases the pallor of his cheeks. The cornea [of his eyes] is yellowish. . . . Spiritually [he is] dead. . . ."

After the halt in Dongo, Mussolini was taken to a frontier post in the mountains above that village. There he talked for a while with the young partisans who held him prisoner before retiring for the night to a small room that served as a cell. But after a few hours he was awakened and told that he was going to be moved elsewhere. "Pedro", the commander of the partisan brigade stationed in Dongo, felt that the mountain post was not sufficiently safe. The partisans were afraid to lose their quarry, for the Allies were looking for the former *duce*; but the general command of the Italian liberation forces had decided that the chief Fascists, those responsible for the long years of moral slavery (and for the defeat of their country), should be captured, held, and judged by Italians.

Accordingly, they took the precaution of bandaging Mussolini's head to make him look like a wounded partisan so that he would not be easily recognised on the way. He raised no objections. "Pedro" and two other partisans— one of them a girl dressed as a nurse—escorted him to a car. It was raining, and the night was chilly. They drove out of the mountains, toward the road along the shore of the lake, the way Mussolini had come the day before. Soon they encountered another car. Both cars stopped, and everyone got out into the darkness. A woman walked towards Mussolini, and he recognised Claretta Petacci. He said: "You here too, *signora*?" Claretta, with the other Italians, had been taken to Dongo. There, in late afternoon, she had met "Pedro", who gave her news of the prisoner. Claretta had at once implored "Pedro" to let her rejoin her lover.

In the very early hours of April 28 the two cars resumed their drive southward through the rain, in the direction of

Menaggio and Como. At 3.30 a.m. the party reached a small house owned by a peasant family known to the partisans and accustomed to guests arriving in the middle of the night. The peasant's wife, who did not recognise Mussolini and his mistress, agreed to let them stay and hurriedly made beds for them in an upstairs room. The room was plain, almost squalid, and in its bareness, in the poverty of its furnishing, it called to mind the room in which Benito had been born over sixty years before. It was as if Fate were announcing that the cycle of Mussolini's life was at a close. Two partisans stood guard outside the room.

The two prisoners got up late in the morning, about 11 o'clock a.m., and ate a meal of must, milk, bread, and salami in their room. At 4 p.m. a partisan officer, "Colonel Valerio", came into their room—his true name was Walter Audisio, and in peacetime he was an accountant. Before coming to the country house, "Valerio" had convened a military escort in Dongo. The court had swiftly tried Mussolini *in absentia* and sentenced him to death. (Also sentenced to die were seventeen of the high Fascists captured by the partisans and brought to Dongo.)

Now "Colonel Valerio" led Mussolini and Claretta Petacci outside and down a steep path to a car. Several partisans accompanied them. The car was driven along a country road and stopped at a place called Giulino di Mezzegra, near the solitary gate of a villa hidden in a cluster of trees. The two prisoners were made to stand against a low wall a few feet from one another. According to one report, Claretta whispered to her lover, "Aren't you glad that I followed you to the end?" "Valerio" read the death sentence to Mussolini, and then he and the other partisans fired. The next day in Milan the two bodies were exposed in Piazzale Loreto, with those of other Fascists executed in Dongo.

LAURA FERMI *Mussolini*

# Venice

OH THE damp silence of Venice, with only human noises and the water swishing against the banks of the canals. Venice has changed less than any other city in the last two hundred years, and the Vandals, who planned it, have been prevented from building a motor road across the city.

This city of hundreds of thousands of inhabitants is the most artificial achievement in all town-building. As basis there are low sandbanks which are strengthened, to bear the weight of the palaces and piazzas, by a whole forest of tree-trunks.

Venice is sometimes called a dead city, for it was once the capital of a great maritime Empire, controlled parts of Greece and all Dalmatia, and held the Turks at bay. Hence Wordsworth wrote:

## On the Extinction of the Venetian Republic

Once did She hold the gorgeous east in fee;
And was the safeguard of the west: the worth
Of Venice did not fall below her birth,
Venice, the eldest Child of Liberty.
She was a maiden City, bright and free;
No guile seduced, no force could violate;
And, when she took unto herself a Mate,
She must espouse the everlasting Sea.
And what if she had seen those glories fade,
Those titles vanish, and that strength decay;
Yet shall some tribute of regret be paid
When her long life hath reached its final day:

Men are we, and must grieve when even the Shade
Of that which once was great is passed away.

WILLIAM WORDSWORTH


And Henry James's picture of over sixty years ago is still valid.


### Air of Venice

Certain little mental pictures rise before the collector of
memories at the simple mention, written or spoken, of the
places he has loved. When I hear, when I see, the magical
name [of Venice] it is not of the great Square that I think,
with its strange basilica and its high arcades, nor of the
wide mouth of the Grand Canal, with the stately steps and
the well-poised dome of the Salute; it is not of the low
lagoon, nor the sweet Piazzetta, nor the dark chambers of
St Mark's. I simply see a narrow canal in the heart of the
city—a patch of green water and a surface of pink wall.
The gondola moves slowly; it gives a great smooth swerve,
passes under a bridge, and the gondolier's cry, carried over
the quiet water, makes a kind of splash in the stillness. A
girl crosses the little bridge, which has an arch like a camel's
back, with an old shawl on her head, which makes her
characteristic and charming; you see her against the sky as
you float beneath. The pink of the old wall seems to fill the
whole place; it sinks even into the opaque water. Behind
the wall is a garden, out of which the long arm of a white
June rose—the roses of Venice are splendid—has flung
itself by way of spontaneous ornament. On the other side
of this small water-way is a great shabby façade of Gothic
windows and balconies—balconies on which dirty clothes
are hung and under which a cavernous-looking doorway
opens from a low flight of slimy water-steps. It is very hot
and still, the canal has a queer smell, and the whole place
is enchanting.

HENRY JAMES Italian Hours

39

# St Mark's

Yet here it still is, all of it: even St Mark's, the cathedral which has had so many escapes. Its latest feat was to survive an Austrian bomb that fell, just outside it, in the 1914-18 war. Not many years before, there had been the collapse of the Campanile, which might have altogether crushed its fragile grey domes. And earlier, some seventy years ago, Ruskin had delivered it from other and not lesser dangers by the fiery eloquence of his prose: for then an actual suggestion had been put forward to pull down the barbaric old thing, as it was at the time believed to be, and rebuild it properly in the best Austrian classical style of the period. So intense, for some reason or other, had been the feeling against it, that the principal English architectural journal of the day devoted a leading article to Ruskin's defence of the church, beginning with the sentence: "Mr Ruskin thinks St Mark's a beautiful church: we consider it an ugly one." But even the restorers, with their more subtle, continual, and calculated efforts at destruction—that slow, relentless, insect-like eating away and rebuilding of a mighty church until a new creation is substituted for the old one which we loved, while all the time it is achieved under the cloak of loudly proclaimed necessity and good intentions, and so gradually carried out that many people notice the havoc being wrought no more than they perceive in progress the slow decay of their own minds and bodies —cannot entirely spoil its enchantment. Indeed, a visitor is bound on every occasion to discover some new and beautiful effect or detail: for not only is the edifice itself an unrivalled work of art, but it is, in addition, a museum of the first order.

It is as though, whenever the Venetians beheld anything anywhere that they deemed of the finest quality, in bronze, marble, porphyry, or crystal, their first thought was, "How can we steal this for St Mark's?" Being an ingenious and bold people, untroubled by scruples, they generally succeeded in discovering a method, albeit sometimes they failed to bring it home safely. Thus the Adriatic coast of

Italy is sprinkled with objects that the Venetians lost at sea, on their way back from Constantinople, and which eventually, and after the Venetians had forgotten about them, were recovered from the waves. Nevertheless, an immense amount of booty reached the city safely: and, once there, the next thought of the Venetians was, "Shall we set it in the façade, or upon the side-walls of our church?" And, by some strange fortune, this haphazard process did actually adorn it. The incongruity of the exhibits is by one means or another banished until they become part of the building, grow in to it, as an orchid flowers from a tropical tree, and even impart to this far shrine a portion of the magic of the places from which they were wrenched.

And what fabulous and fantastic objects, even though familiarity has somewhat dimmed their marvel for us, compose this proud plunder; the four bronze horses which are supposed to have pawed, when first cast, upon the top of Nero's triumphal march and alone, out of all the stamping, bronze chariot-horses of the antique world, remain to our age—and, moreover, alone of all such creatures, in this horse-free city, here represent the equine race; the four snub-nosed porphyry kings, ancient and obscure, at the corner near the Doge's palace, thus displayed for ever in ritual embrace. . . . And then the Treasury is a museum of smaller objects. There are crystal vases, jade vases, jewelled Byzantine book-covers, and gold and silver vessels, many of which are so unlike all else that it is difficult to assign to them a period or nationality; some are Sassanian and Chinese presents to the Emperors of the East, while others are the native products of Greek magnificence. Indeed, this small space contains more relics of the Eastern Empire, of that perished system which for a thousand years *was* civilisation, than any museum of the world; solely here is it possible to appraise, by means of this wonderful jewellery, a vanished culture, to conjecture, on the same plane, the other objects that must have existed, and thus for a moment to obtain a perspective of the loveliness of palace life in the Great City, before the Crusaders—chiefly urged on to it, alas! by the Venetians—sacked it and, in so doing, weakened for ever its power and prestige, thereby pre-ordaining its subsequent and awful fate. . . . But the jealousy of the Venetians was useless: after once you have visited Constantinople and have seen Santa Sophia, even in its present desolate and humiliating state when it is dead and dreary, when everything that could impair its beauty has been achieved and no indignity has been spared it, yet for ever afterwards St Mark's in Venice, lovely creation though it is, will seem an upstart, a usurping poor relation grown rich through the plunder of those who should have been dear to her.

OSBERT SITWELL *Winters of Content*

Henry James and Sir Osbert Sitwell were only two of the innumerable foreigners and Italians who came to Venice, admired, and stayed. Richard Wagner died there. Gabriele D'Annunzio wrote a novel about Venice as encrusted with ornaments as the palaces themselves. For Byron Venice was the scene of one of his love affairs that shocked his fellow-countrymen —with Teresa Guiccioli. This is how he saw the city.

### *Venice*

I stood in Venice, on the Bridge of Sighs;
A palace and a prison on each hand:
I saw from out the wave her structures rise
As from the stroke of the enchanter's wand:
A thousand years their cloudy wings expand
Around me, and a dying Glory smiles
O'er the far times, when many a subject land
Look'd to the winged Lion's marble piles,
Where Venice sat in state, throned on her hundred isles!

She looks a sea Cybele, fresh from ocean,
Rising with her tiara of proud towers
At airy distance, with majestic motion,
A ruler of the waters and their powers:

And such she was;—her daughters had their dowers
From spoils of nations, and the exhaustless East
Pour'd in her lap all gems in sparkling showers.
In purple was she robed, and of her feast
Monarchs partook, and deem'd their dignity increased.
LORD BYRON Childe Harold's Pilgrimage

I must be allowed to quote the following from a contemporary poet, which nowadays gives me more pleasure than Byron. The *dogana* is the old Customs House.

## *On the Dogana's Steps*

I sat on the Dogana's steps
For the gondolas cost too much, that year,
And there were not *those girls,* there was one face,
And the Buccentoro twenty yards off, howling *Stretti,*
And the lit cross-beams, that year, in the Morosini,
And peacocks in Koré's house, or there may have been.
    Gods float in the azure air,
Bright gods and Tuscan, back before dew was shed.
Light: and the first light, before ever dew was fallen.
Panisks, and from the oak, dryas,
And from the apple, maelid,
Through all the wood, and the leaves are full of voices,
A-whisper, and the clouds bow over the lake,
And there are gods upon them,
And in the water, the almond-white swimmers,
The silvery water glazes the upturned nipple,
    As Poggio has remarked.
Green veins in the turquoise.
Or: the gray steps lead up under the cedars.
EZRA POUND Canto III

The most eccentric of all English-speaking writers who became a Venetian was Frederick Rolfe, Baron Corvo, worshipper

of the Borgias (and of street boys) and author of *Hadrian VII*.
Unfortunately Corvo was more than a mere enhancer, he was a
congenital liar. This is how he described his halcyon days in
Venice.

### Venetian Euphoria

I came to Venice in August for a six weeks' holiday; and
lived and worked and slept in my *barchetta* almost always.
It seemed that, by staying on, I could most virtuously and
most righteously cheat autumn and winter. Such was the
effect of this kind of Venetian life on me, that I felt no more
than twenty-five years old, in everything excepting value-
less experience and valuable disillusion. The bounding joy
of vigorous health, the physical capacity for cheerful (nay,
gay) endurance, the careless, untroubled mental activity,
the perfectly gorgeous appetite, the prompt, delicate,
dreamless nights of sleep, which betoken healthy youth—
all this (with indescribable happiness) I had triumphantly
snatched from solitude with the sun and the sea. I went
swimming half a dozen times a day, beginning at white
dawn, and ending after sunsets which set the whole lagoon
ablaze with amethyst and topaz. Between friends, I will
confess that I am not guiltless of often getting up in the
night and popping silently overboard to swim for an hour
in the clear of a great gold moon—*plenilunio*—or among the
waving reflections of the stars. (O my goodness me, how
heavenly a spot that is!) When I wanted change of scene
and anchorage, I rowed with my two *gondoglieri*; and there
is nothing known to physiculturalists (for giving you
"poise" and the organs and figure of a slim young Diady-
menos) like rowing standing in the Mode Venetian. It is
jolly hard work; but no other exercise bucks you up as
does springing forward from your toe-tips and stretching
forward to the full in pushing the oar, or produces such
exquisite lassitude at night when your work is done. And I
wrote quite easily for a good seven hours each day. Could
anything be more felicitous?

And, one day, I replenished my stock of provisions at

44

Burano; and at sunset we rowed away to find a station for the night. Imagine a twilight world of cloudless sky and smoothest sea, all made of warm, liquid, limpid heliotrope and violet and lavender, with bands of burnished copper set with emeralds, melting, on the other hand, into the fathomless blue of the eyes of the prides of peacocks, where the moon rose, rosy as mother-of-pearl. Into such glory we three advanced the black *barchetta*, solemnly, silently, when the last echo of *Ave Maria* died.

Slowly we came out north of Burano into the open lagoon; and rowed eastward to meet the night, as far as the point marked by five *pali*, where the wide canal curves to the south. Slowly we went. There was something so holy —so majestically holy—in that evening silence, that I would not have it broken even by the quiet plash of oars. I was lord of time and place. No engagements cried to be kept. I could go when and where I pleased, fast or slow, far or near. And I chose the near and the slow. I did more. So unspeakably gorgeous was the peace on the lagoon just then, that it inspired me with a lust for doing nothing at all but sitting and absorbing impressions motionlessly. That way come thoughts, new, generally noble.

The wide canal, in which we drifted, is a highway. I have never seen it unspeckled by the *sandali* of Buranelli fishers. Steam-boats and tank-barges of fresh water for Burano, and the ordinary barks of carriage, disturb it, not always, but often. My wish was to find a small canal, away—away. We were (as I said) at the southern side, at the southward curve marked by five *pali*. Opposite, on the other bank, begins the long line of *pali* which shows the deep-water way right down to the Ricevitoria of Treporti; and there, at the beginning of the line, I spied the mouth of a canal which seemed likely to suit me. We rowed across to it, and entered. It tended north-eastward for two or three hundred metres, and then bended like an elbow north-westward. It looked quite a decent canal, perhaps forty metres in width, between sweet mud-banks clothed with sea-lavender about two-foot lengths above high-water mark in places. We pushed inshore, near to the inner bank at the elbow, stuck a couple of oars into the mud fore and aft, and moored there.

Baicolo and Caicio got out the draught board and cigarettes, and played below their breath on the *puppa*; while I sat still, bathing my soul in peace, till the night was dark and Selene high in the limpid sapphire-blue. Then they lighted the *fanali*, and put up the impermeable awning with wings and curtains to cover the whole *barchetta*; and made a parmentier soup to eat with our wine and *polenta*. And, when kapok-cushions had been arranged on the floor, and summer sleeping bags laid over them, we took our last dash overboard, said our prayers, and went to bed. Baicolo at *prova* with his feet towards mine amidships, and Caicio under the *puppa* with his feet well clear of my pillowed head. So, we slept.

Soon after sunrise I awakened: it was a sunrise of opal and fire: the boys were deep in slumber. I took down the awning, and unmoored quietly, and mounted the *puppa* to row about in the dewy freshness in search of a fit place for my morning plunge. I am very particular about this. Deep water I must have—as deep as possible—I being what the Venetians call *appassionato per l'acqua*. Beside that, I have a vehement dyspathy against getting entangled in weeds or mud, to make my toe-nails dirtier than my finger-nails. And, being congenitally myopic, I see more clearly in deep water than in shallow, almost as clearly, in fact, as with a concave monocle on land. So I left the *barchetta* to drift with the current, while I took soundings with the long oar of the *puppa*, in several parts of the canal, near both banks as well as in the middle. Nowhere could I touch bottom and this signified that my bathing place was more than four metres in depth. Needless to say that I gave a joyful morning yell, which dragged from sleep the luxury-loving Baicolo to make coffee, and the faithful dog Caicio to take my oar and keep the *barchetta* near me; and then I plunged overboard to revel in the limpid green water. Lord, how lovely is Thy smooth salt water flowing on flesh!

A. J. A. SYMONS *The Quest for Corvo*

But things were always going wrong with Corvo. He quarrelled with almost everyone he knew and ran up debts at the Hotel Cavaletto where he lived in a grand manner. What follows is typical of the other side of the picture.

## An Awful State

My dear Man:

I'm in an awful state; and I firmly believe that I'm finished if I don't get relief *instanter*.

The last fortnight has been a chapter of misfortunes. I've been literally fighting for life through a series of storms. Do you realise what that means in a little boat, leaky and so coated with weed and barnacles by a summer's use, that it is almost too heavy to move with the oar, and behaves like an inebriate in winds or weather? I assure you it's no joke. And storms get up on this lagoon in ten minutes, leaving no time to make a port. I'm frequently struggling for 50-60 hours on end. Results: I've lost about 300 pages of my new MS of *Hubert's Arthur*. Parts were oiled by a lamp blown over them: winds and waves carried away the rest. At every possible minute I am re-writing them: but, horrible to say, grey mists float about my eye-corners just through sheer exhaustion. The last few days I have been anchored near an empty island, Sacca Fisola, not too far away from civilisation to be out of reach of fresh water, but only enough for dying alone in the boat if need be. Well, to show you how worn out I am, I frankly say that I have funked it. This is my dilemma. I'll be quite plain about it. If I stay out on the lagoon, the boat will sink, I shall swim perhaps for a few hours, and then I shall be eaten alive by crabs. At low water every mudbank swarms with them. If I stay anchored near an island, I must keep continually awake: for, the moment I cease moving, I am invaded by swarms of swimming rats, who in the winter are so voracious that they attack even a man who is motionless. I have tried it. And have been bitten. Oh my dear man you can't think how artful fearless ferocious they are. I rigged

47

up two bits of chain, lying loose on my prow and poop with a string by which I could shake them when attacked. For two nights the dodge acted. The swarms came (up the anchor rope) and nuzzled me: I shook the chains: the beasts plopped overboard. Then they got used to the noise and sneered. Then they bit the strings. Then they bit my toes and woke me shrieking and shaking with fear.

Now this is what I have done. I am perfectly prepared to persevere to the end. So I have taken the boat to a *squero* to be repaired. This will take a fortnight. When she is seaworthy again, I'll go out and face my fate with her. Meanwhile I'm running a tick on the Cavalletto, simply that I may eat and sleep and write hard at restoring the 300 odd pages of *Hubert's Arthur*. When that is done, the boat will be ready. I will assign that MS to you and send it.

My dear man, I am so awfully lonely. And tired. Is there no chance of setting me straight?

Ever yours R.

A. J. A. SYMONS *The Quest for Corvo*

In his novel about Venice called *Il Fuoco,* or The Fire, D'Annunzio exalted Venetian art and especially Giorgione to the pinnacles of heaven. Here are two comments by Americans in a quieter mood.

### *Venetian Painting*

I had been curious to see whether in the galleries and temples of Venice I should be disposed to transpose my old estimates—to burn what I had adored and adore what I had burned. It is a sad truth that one can stand in the Ducal Palace for the first time but once, with the deliciously ponderous sense of that particular half-hour's being an era in one's mental history; but I had the satisfaction of finding at least—a great comfort in a short stay—that none of my early memories were likely to change places and that I could take up my admirations where I had left them. I still found Carpaccio delightful, Veronese magnificent, Titian supremely beautiful and Tintoret scarce to be appraised. I repaired immediately to the little church of San Cassano, which contains the smaller of Tintoret's two great Crucifixions; and when I had looked at it awhile I drew a long breath and felt I could now face any other picture in Venice with proper self-possession. It seemed to me I had advanced to the uttermost limit of painting; that beyond this another art—inspired poetry—begins, and that Bellini, Veronese, Giorgione, and Titian, all joining hands and straining every muscle of their genius, reach forward not so far but that they leave a visible space in which Tintoret alone is master. I well remember the exaltations to which he lifted me when first I learned to know him; but the glow of that comparatively youthful amazement is dead, and with it, I fear, that confident vivacity of phrase of which, in trying to utter my impressions, I felt less the magniloquence than the impotence. In his power there are many weak spots, mysterious lapses and fitful intermissions; but when the list of his faults is complete he still remains to me the most *interesting* of painters. His reputation rests chiefly on a more superficial sort of merit—his energy, his unsurpassed productivity, his being, as Théophile Gautier says, *le roi des fougueux*. These qualities are immense, but the great source of his impressiveness is that his indefatigable hand never drew a line that was not, as one may say, a moral line. No painter ever had such breadth and such depth; and even Titian, beside him, scarce figures as more than a great decorative artist. Mr Ruskin, whose eloquence in dealing with the great Venetians sometimes outruns his discretion, is fond of speaking even of Veronese as a painter of deep spiritual intentions. This, it seems to me, is pushing matters too far, and the author of "The Rape of Europa" is, pictorially speaking, no greater casuist than any other genius of supreme good taste. Titian was assuredly a mighty poet, but Tintoret—well, Tintoret was almost a prophet. Before his greatest works you are conscious of a sudden evaporation of old doubts and dilemmas, and the eternal problem of the conflict between idealism and realism dies the most natural of deaths. In his genius the problem is practically solved; the

49

alternatives are so harmoniously interfused that I defy the keenest critic to say where one begins and the other ends. The homeliest prose melts into the most ethereal poetry— the literal and the imaginative fairly confound their identity.

HENRY JAMES Italian Hours

## *Giorgione*

Giorgione's life was short, and very few of his works— not a score in all—have escaped destruction. But these suffice to give us a glimpse into that brief moment when the Renaissance found its most genuine expression in painting. Its over-boisterous passions had quieted down into a sincere appreciation of beauty and of human relations. It would be really hard to say more about Giorgione than this, that his pictures are the perfect reflex of the Renaissance at its height. His works, as well as those of his contemporaries and followers, still continue to be appreciated most by people whose attitude of mind and spirit has most in common with the Renaissance, or by those who look upon Italian art not merely as art, but as the product of this period. For that is its greatest interest. Other schools have accomplished much more in mere painting than the Italian. A serious student of art will scarcely think of putting many of even the highest achievements of the Italians, considered purely as technique, beside the work of the great Dutchmen, the great Spaniard, or even the masters of today. Our real interest in Italian painting is at bottom an interest in that art which we almost instinctively feel to have been the fittest expression found by a period in the history of modern Europe which has much in common with youth. The Renaissance has the fascination of those years when we seemed so full of promise both to ourselves and to everybody else.

BERNHARD BERENSON<br>The Italian Painters of the Renaissance

The Adriatic sea, into which the lagoons of Venice open out, is no longer the desert it was a hundred years ago. The hundred miles of beach on the Italian side is sprawled with bathing establishments, motor cars, and extenuated bodies of the bourgeoisie "getting brown".

## The Adriatic

Poor Adriatic! When will you see again the glories of the Roman fleets of Brindisi, the Liburnian longships and the galleys of Venice? Today your surges beat, wild and stormy, upon two almost deserted coasts and the marshy lowlands of Puglia face the de-populated mountains of Albania. Venice, a tavern, and Trieste, a shop, are not enough to console your shores for their desolation, and the dawn that every day smoothes down your white-maned billows searches vainly along your shores for aught save ruins and memories.

❈ ❈ ❈ ❈ ❈

Memories, memories, always memories across those waves ever restless and unchanging, of those gentle breezes always sweet and perfumed, over that land eternally insatiable and fecund. The Orient has produced over long ages a civilisation that decays in folly; the North has for three hundred years behaved with the infantile pride of one who thinks himself full grown and is perhaps not yet born. Italy has twice surpassed the Orient and forestalled the North, twice was queen and mistress of the world, a miracle of fruitfulness, of power and of disaster. The fires still rage deep within her, despite the elegies of Lamartine or the lack of faith of the pessimists; one day she will overtake those who stand but a pace before her and believe they have advanced a thousand miles. One pace, one pace; no more, I assure you; yet it is a long pace to take.

IPPOLITO NIEVO *The Castle of Fratta*


Padua, on the mainland near Venice, is the seat of one of the oldest universities in the world. Much of what Ippolito Nievo

51

wrote about it a hundred years ago would have been true of Oxford at the same time.

## Padua University

My life in Padua was really that of a poor student. I looked like the servant of some priest and bore modestly the symbols of the Italian nation as was still the custom of students, as it had been in the times of Galileo, when Greeks, Spaniards, English, Germans, Poles, and Norwegians competed at this university. It was said that Gustavus Adolphus was there a disciple of the great astronomer; which was of very little importance in the destiny either of the one or of the other. My companions at college were for the most part mountain boors, coarse, dirty, ignorant, the seed-bed of future chancellors for those proud magistrates or of venal notaries for the criminal courts. They caroused and squabbled among themselves and picked continual quarrels with the police, the butchers or the innkeepers; above all with these last, since they had the strange idea of not allowing anyone to leave the taverns before they had paid their bills. These disputes ended before the privileged tribunal of the students, where the judges showed the easy good sense of always giving judgement in favour of the students, in order not to incur their wrath, as implacable as it was lacking in justice and moderation. The patrician students kept as aloof as possible from this rabble, more from fear than from pride, I imagine. And there was not lacking a middle class, also, that of the majority, of the waverers, of the moderates, who during the fat days of the month took part in the expensive pleasures of the nobles, and in the last lean days had recourse to the villainous and impudent junketings of the others. They spoke ill of these with the others and of the others with these; afterwards among themselves, they mocked at both of them. They were the real precursors of that middle class, brainless and heartless, who considered themselves democrats since they were equally unable to obey nobly as to command usefully.

IPPOLITO NIEVO *The Castle of Fratta*

# On the Road

THE ITALIANS are passionate drivers, with quick reactions, a taste for speed and a certain amount of ruthlessness. The technique of driving, either on the great autostradas or on the winding climbing roads through the Alps or the Apennines or the Tuscan hills, is different indeed from the English queue. Despite the roads, the mountains are still wild. And anyone who travels from the great northern plain into Tuscany may pause and think —while he is wondering whether to pass an *autotreno* (a long truck with a long trailer)—on the difficulties that confronted his ancestors.

## *Brigands in the Apennines*

Some two years since, it began to be perceived, both in Bologna and in Florence, that travellers who took the road upon which we were now embarked showed a strange tendency to vanish. The enquiries which were set on foot by the two spineless governments concerned succeeded only in establishing one fact beyond dispute, namely, that no trace of human remains was ever discovered among the ridges of the Appennine. One evening, a Spanish traveller and his wife were obliged by the raging snow-storm which had overtaken them to seek the shelter of an ill-famed tavern in Pietra Mala—this same village where we now find ourselves. It would be hard to conceive a more squalid and unprepossessing hovel; yet the hostess, so the travellers remarked, wore diamond rings, which ill-accorded with her ogre-ish appearance. This woman told the travellers that she would send a servant to borrow white bed-linen from

53

the priest, whose dwelling lay some three miles distant from the inn. The Spaniard's young wife being scared almost to death by the sinister aspect of the tavern, her husband, pretexting that he desired to fetch a handkerchief from the coach outside, made signs to the *vetturino* [coachman], and managed, without being observed from within the building, to hold a certain conversation with him; incidentally, this fellow too, who had heard rumours and to spare concerning travellers who had vanished, was in no better state, if not in a worse, than his passengers. Rapidly, they agreed together upon a plan. In the full hearing of the hostess, the Spaniard advised the *vetturino* that he and his wife should be awakened at an hour not later than five o'clock the following morning; after which, having let it be understood that they both felt unwell, the travelling couple ate no more than a few mouthfuls at the supper-table, and retired immediately to their room; here they waited, half expiring with terror and straining their ears for the least noise, until every sound within the house had ceased; and so at last, about an hour after midnight, they made their escape and fled to join the *vetturino*, who was already waiting at the appointed place, the better part of a mile from the tavern, with his horses and his coach.

Upon his safe return to Florence, the *vetturino* poured out the tale of his alarms to his own master, signor Polastro, a man of scrupulous honour. Urged on by the insistence of the latter, the police made strenuous efforts, and after many failures, arrested a certain vagabond creature who was observed to haunt this particular tavern in Pietra Mala. Under the threat of immediate execution, he revealed to his captors that the priest—a man named Biondi, the same to whom the hostess was accustomed to send out to borrow bed-linen—was the chief among this band of brigands, whose practice it was to descend upon the inn towards two o'clock in the morning, at which hour it might be expected that the travellers would be sound asleep in their beds. There was always a grain or two of opium in the wine which was served at supper. The rule of the gang was to murder both the travellers and the *vetturino*; after which deed, the robbers would stow the corpses away once more inside their own carriage, harness the horses, and drag it to some deserted spot among the high peaks of the Appennine. Once this chosen place was reached, the horses likewise would be slaughtered, while the coach, the travellers, and all their private effects would be destroyed in one grim funeral pyre; nothing, strictly *nothing*, would be preserved, save only gold, silver and precious stones. The corpses and the charred remnants of the vehicle would be buried with meticulous care, while watches and jewellery would be sold in distant Genoa. Alerted at long last by this confession, the police managed to entrap the whole gang as its members sat all unawares about a sumptuous banquet laid for them in the presbytery and presided over by Biondi; only that worthy lady, the hostess of the tavern, was not present; and she, whose task it was, by sending out for the sheets, to warn the gang that travellers worthy of attention had recently descended at the inn, was discovered at home in her own lair.

STENDHAL *Rome, Naples and Florence*

Plenty of middle-aged men still remember the chaotic days of wartime. During the German occupation of Italy it was right and noble to be a brigand—men threw themselves into irregular warfare with reckless courage. Hundreds upon hundreds of escaped Allied prisoners of war lived with the bands of partisans.

## Partisan Warfare

We attacked on a hot June day. The woods were heavy with sunshine. Beetles came drifting over the bushes like Bombers. There were six of us—the major, myself, four South Africans. We came to the edge of the wood and saw the bivouac tent a couple of hundred yards away across an open field of grass. There was no movement. They would be asleep in the shade or in the back of the truck. We climbed a fence and jumped down among the trailing branches of a briar. A thorn whipped back and struck a South African in the eye-ball. He dropped his Sten and clapped a hand to his eye. There was a report as the jolt of the fall brought the firing pin forward on to the cartridge. At the edge of the wood a couple of figures in bathing trunks rose and peered across through the sunshine. We ran forward with a shout. They had their hands up—boys caught in a wave of fear that melted their guts and loosened their sphincters. I looked for the other two. One was by the truck in a little nest of branches he had made for shelter from the sun. He was scrambling for a weapon. I shouted in German not to be a fool. He stood up with a grenade in his hand and tugged at the thong which would arm the fuse. When I fired he was a couple of yards away. Two shots from the Beretta. One after the other. I saw two little marks appear on his belly, just above his bathing trunks. He clapped his hands over them and fell on his back. You idiot, I said, and bent over him. His face blenched under the sunburn. He groaned a little and twisted about as if to shake off his death. Then he half sat up, looked at my face, and seized my hand, clinging to it like a frightened child. I laid him back and freed myself from his grasp. My hand was sticky with his blood. Beyond the woods the fourth of them was running through the fields, doubling and ducking. At that range there was no point in trying to catch him or to bring him down.

In the truck we found small arms ammunition—the wrong calibre—mortar bombs, and new-fangled anti-tank weapons we didn't know how to use. The wounded man lay in the shade and groaned.

We made the other two carry him and set off through the woods. In a safe spot we rested and waited for evening. He was silent now, his face a strange ashen hue. There was no haemorrhage, only a little dark blood oozing from the two holes. The flesh had closed again over the bullets. We covered him with a blanket and got water to bathe the sweat from his face. His mates sat together and watched and did not talk. After dusk a peasant cart came with a mattress and jolted him along the tracks to the nearest farmhouse. We laid him in the barn in the straw and covered him well. From time to time he would open his eyes and oolk at

*Venice: Palladio's church of San Giorgio. The island of San Giorgio once housed a monastery, then a barracks. Now one can have peaceful strolls in the garden in the cool of the evening*

*Venice amid the dead canals*

*Florence: The Middle Ages and the Renaissance
still live side by side in almost every street*

*Florence: The Perseus holding the severed head of the Medusa is probably Benvenuto Cellini's best-known work. One can sit in the shade of the loggia and look at it for hours*

me with incredulity. A fair-haired boy with a good face lying in the mucky sweat of death.

When I went in the others were all round the table eating supper. I spoke with the boys and told them not to be afraid. Unless they did anything stupid they were safe. A doctor was coming for the one outside.

He came towards midnight, looked, felt his pulse, shrugged. "There's not much to be done about it," he said. "I'll give him an injection for his heart. He may last the night. Even if you got him to a hospital there's not much hope."

A South African came and stood beside us.

"What does he say?"

"He says there's not much hope. Maybe we could leave him by the roadside tomorrow with a note. There's bound to be a convoy."

The boy stirred, opened his eyes and looked up at me in the light of the lantern.

"Will I die?" he asked in English. "Will I die?"

I told him what we would do. He shut his eyes and slept.

In the morning he was worse; his breathing was laboured and irregular. Caravaggio came to report that parachutists had been dropped to us—Italian saboteurs from Bari. I took a last look at the boy and went off through the woods. I had gone about a mile when from the direction of the farm-house I heard three bursts of fire.

※ ※ ※ ※ ※ ※

*They are buried on the major's estate in the midst of high broom. The peasant who kept the stud bull showed me the spot, leading me down through the bushes with an air of mystery. We came to a little open patch. The broom was high above our heads. The air was full of the rumour of insects. "Who?" I asked. "The three Germans." The air between the bushes was hot, still and aromatic. "Poor things," I said, using the Italian formula, "they too were sons of mothers." "What do you mean 'poor things'," he said. "We didn't kill enough of them."*

STUART HOOD *Pebbles From My Skull*

But even today there are oases of quietness and contemplation. Village life is as stable in Italy as anywhere in the world. Here is a description of what seems to me almost the ideal way of existing. Readers may be surprised that my quotation is from Machiavelli: but like most of us Machiavelli had two or more characters. In the country, peace and tranquillity descended on him, he sublimated his obsession with power into a poetic contemplation of the power of men of the ancient world long dead, and so came into harmony with the universe.

### Village Life

I rise in the morning with the sun, and I go off to a wood of mine which I am having cut down, where I stop for two hours to see what was done the day before and to talk to the woodcutters who always have some trouble on hand either among themselves or with their neighbours. . . . Leaving the wood I go to a spring and thence to some bird-traps of mine. I have a book with me, Dante or Petrarch or one of the minor poets, Tibullus, Ovid or the like. I read about their amorous passions and their loves, I remember my own, and dwell enjoyably on these thoughts for a while. Then I go on to the road and into the tavern. I talk to the passers-by, I ask what news of their villages, I hear all sorts of things, and observe the various tastes and ideas of men. In the meanwhile it is time for dinner, and with my folk I eat what food this poor farm and miserable patrimony of mine provides. When I have eaten I go back to the tavern. Here I find the host, and usually a butcher, a miller, and a couple of kilnmen. With them I degrade myself playing all day at *cricca* and tric-trac, and this gives rise to a thousand arguments and endless vexations with insulting words, and most times there is a fight over a penny, and we can be heard shouting from as far away as San Casciano. And so, surrounded by these lice, I blow the cobwebs out of my brain and relieve the unkindness of my fate, content that she trample on me in this way to see if she is not ashamed to treat me thus.

When evening comes I return home and go into my study,

and at the door I take off my daytime dress covered in mud and dirt, and put on royal and curial robes; and then decently attired I enter the courts of the ancients, where affectionately greeted by them, I partake of that good which is mine alone and for which I was born; where I am not ashamed to talk with them and inquire the reasons of their actions; and they out of their human kindness answer me, and for four hours at a stretch I feel no worry of any kind; I forget all my troubles, I am not afraid of poverty or of death. I give myself up entirely to them. And because Dante says that understanding does not constitute knowledge unless it is retained in the memory, I have written down what I have learned from their conversation and composed a short work, *de Principatibus*.

ROBERTO RIDOLFI The Life of Niccolò Machiavelli

Italy is such a delightful place to live in if you happen to be a man. There one may enjoy that exquisite luxury of Socialism—that true Socialism which is based not on equality of income or character, but on the equality of manners. In the democracy of the *caffè* or the street the great question of our life has been solved, and the brotherhood of man is a reality. But it is accomplished at the expense of the sisterhood of women. Why should you not make friends with your neighbour at the theatre or in the train, when you know and he knows that feminine criticism and feminine insight and feminine prejudice will never come between you ! Though you become as David and Jonathan, you need never enter his home, nor he yours. All your lives you will meet under the open air, the only roof-tree of the South, under which he will spit and swear, and you will drop your h's, and nobody will think the worse of either.

Meanwhile the women—they have, of course, their house and their church, with its admirable and frequent services, to which they are escorted by the maid. Otherwise they do not go out much, for it is not genteel to walk, and you are too poor to keep a carriage. Occasionally you will take them to the *caffè* or theatre, and immediately all your wonted

acquaintance there desert you, except those few who are
expecting to marry into your family. It is all very sad. But
one consolation emerges—life is very pleasant in Italy if
you are a man.

E. M. FORSTER *Where Angels Fear To Tread*


That was written over half a century ago. Nowadays Rome is
full of women drivers, and young men are too blasé to follow an
unaccompanied girl in the streets muttering caresses and admiring
her legs and hair. Of course in southern Italy women are still
kept very much at home, and one can know a man for years
without meeting his womenfolk. Yet these women make up for
their apartheid and obtain their power in another way. The
mamma by the cooking pot is the centre of all life for her offspring,
she is the earth-mother. Italians are mamma-worshippers, and I
have sometimes thought this may explain their special devotion
to the Madonna.


But there is another side to Italian country life—the Italian
garden. Machiavelli—though less than Petrarch, the *arch*-
romantic—had a love of nature. But the stronger tradition in
Italy is a certain *distrust* of nature. Nature is like an animal—best
when it is tamed. So the Italian garden is as truly a piece of
architecture as the Italian church. It is laid out in squares and
pavements, it has fountains and a riot of statues, like the Villa
d'Este at Tivoli. The very prose of my next quotation is inspired
by this delightful sense of artifice.


### The Life of the Young Lords and Ladies at the Villa After Mass at Santa Maria Novella

. . . Whereupon Pampinea rose, and said gaily:—"Here
are gardens, meads, and other places delightsome enough,
where you may wander at will, and take your pleasure; but
on the stroke of tierce, let all be here to breakfast in the
shade."

Thus dismissed by their new queen the gay company

sauntered gently through a garden, the young men saying sweet things to the fair ladies, who wove fair garlands of divers sorts of leaves and sang love-songs.

Having thus spent the time allowed them by the queen, they returned to the house, where they found that Parmeno had entered on his office with zeal; for in a hall on the ground-floor they saw tables covered with the whitest of cloths, and beakers that shone like silver, and sprays of broom scattered everywhere. So, at the bidding of the queen, they washed their hands, and all took their places as marshalled by Parmeno. Dishes, daintily prepared, were served, and the finest wines were at hand; the three serving-men did their office noiselessly; in a word all was fair and ordered in a seemly manner; whereby the spirits of the company rose, and they seasoned their viands with pleasant jests and sprightly sallies. Breakfast done, the tables were removed, and the queen bade fetch instruments of music; for all, ladies and young men alike, knew how to tread a measure, and some of them played and sang with great skill: so, at her command, Dioneo having taken a lute, and Fiammetta a viol, they struck up a dance in sweet concert; and, the servants being dismissed to their repast, the queen, attended by the other ladies and the two young men, led off a stately carol; which ended they fell to singing ditties dainty and gay. Thus they diverted themselves until the queen, deeming it time to retire to rest, dismissed them all for the night. So the three young men and the ladies withdrew to their several quarters, which were in different parts of the palace. There they found the beds well made, and abundance of flowers, as in the hall; and so they undressed, and went to bed.

Shortly after noon the queen rose, and roused the rest of the ladies, as also the young men, averring that it was injurious to the health to sleep long in the daytime. They therefore hied them to a meadow, where the grass grew green and luxuriant, being nowhere scorched by the sun, and a light breeze gently fanned them.

BOCCACCIO *The Decameron*

Here is something more immediate to look out for on the road.

## *Sport*

More perhaps than even football, the national sport of Italy is bicycle-racing, and the baffled motorist will often find himself held up by traffic police or even find a main road closed for hours, waiting for a stream of skinny cyclists in multicoloured jerseys to come pedalling desperately past, preceded and followed by gaggles of cars and motor-bicycles and traffic police. Considering that only a few spectators can see the finish, it is difficult to understand why this sport should arouse an enthusiasm on the Continent comparable with that of cricket in England and bullfighting in Spain. But then, any but the most insular of Englishmen must admit in all fairness that it is not easy to understand the cricket enthusiast either, while Central Europeans, it is credibly reported, will sit for days excitedly watching a chess match. Sport is perhaps the classic example of *de gustibus non est disputandum*.

For the ten years after the War, the gulf between Communists and Christian Democrats was hardly deeper than that between Bartolists and Coppists—a sort of dual division like that between the Green and the Blue factions in the Hippodrome of Byzantium, which paralleled, cut across and probably even surpassed that between the Orthodox and the Monophysites. Bartoli and Coppi were the rival cycling champions, and the walls of Italy were covered with inscriptions—*W* or *M Coppi* or *Bartali*, as the case might be. These mystic letters mean *Viva* or *Morte*, which should be translated in our own less dramatic idiom as "Long live" or "Down with". It is at first rather unnerving to walk about the streets and see them smeared with "Death to Rome" and "Death to Latium". One imagines the capital of Latium to be crawling with masked Nihilists until one realises that *M la Roma* and *M la Lazio* refer to the rival local football teams and are the work of some *tifoso* of its rival, much as a cockney fan might chalk up "Down with Arsenal" or "Up the Spurs".

ARCHIBALD LYALL *Rome Sweet Rome*

# Florence and Tuscany

HILLY TUSCANY is the ancestral home of Italian poets and painters. Many of the great poets, Dante, Petrarch, Boccaccio, came from here; so did Giotto and Fra Angelico, Leonardo da Vinci and Michelangelo. The best time to visit Florence is in the spring or the autumn. In summer it is stiflingly hot. Winter is a good time for visiting the churches and art galleries—granting one is assured of proper heating in one's bedroom. Italians endure cold far more easily than heat and their ideas of winter warmth are polar for Englishmen, not to mention Americans.

## Tuscan Landscape

Milan is a riverless city, circular in shape, set in the centre of a plain, whose level expanse, devoid of undulation, is threaded by a hundred streamlets of fresh-running water. Florence, by contrast, lies in the hollow of a narrowish valley cut deep in the rampart of hills which flank it on the south. This latter city, which, by the pattern of her streets, is in some ways reminiscent of Paris, is set astride the Arno much as Paris is built astride the Seine. Likewise the Arno— a mere mountain torrent, artificially swollen, by means of a transverse causeway constructed to work a mill-wheel, to the dimensions of a self-respecting river beneath the bridges of Florence—flows from east to west. If you mount the southern hillside, climbing through the gardens of the *Palazzo Pitti* and from thence embarking upon a circuit of the walls as far as the highroad to Arezzo, you may gain some notion of the countless multitude of little hills which compose the domain of Tuscany; carpeted with olive-groves, with vineyards and with narrow strips of cereal, the undulating surface of the land is cultivated like a garden. And indeed, agriculture is a pursuit most admirably suited to the placid, pacific, husbanding genius of the Tuscan race.

The landscape—just as we may observe it in paintings by Leonardo or by Raphael in his early manner—often terminates in a perspective of dark foliage against the clear blue of a cloudless sky.

STENDHAL Rome, Naples and Florence

Tuscany is especially flowery, being wetter than Sicily and more homely than the Roman hills. Tuscany manages to remain so remote, and secretly smiling to itself in its many sleeves. There are so many hills popping up, and they take no notice of one another. There are so many little deep valleys with streams that seem to go their own little way entirely, regardless of river and sea. There are thousands, millions of utterly secluded little nooks, though the land has been under cultivation these thousands of years. But the intensive culture of vine and olive and wheat, by the ceaseless industry of naked human hands and winter-shod feet, and slow stepping, soft-eyed oxen does not devastate a country, does not denude it, does not lay it bare, does not uncover its nakedness, does not drive away either Pan or his children. The streams run and rattle over wild rocks of secret places, and murmur through blackthorn thickets where the nightingales sing all together, unruffled and undaunted.

It is queer that a country so perfectly cultivated as Tuscany, where half the produce of five acres of land will have to support ten human mouths, still has so much room for the wild flowers and the nightingale. When little hills heave themselves suddenly up, and shake themselves free of neighbours, man has to build his garden and his vineyard, and sculp his landscape. Talk of hanging gardens of Babylon, all Italy, apart from the plains, is a hanging garden. For centuries upon centuries man has been patiently modelling the surface of the Mediterranean countries, gently

*Siena still looks back to the Middle Ages, her age of art and greatness. The medieval costumes come out on festival days. They are of the same age as the churches*

*In Tuscany, where this picture comes from, little girls at
their first communions sometimes also wear angels' wings*

rounding the hills, and graduating the big slopes and the little slopes into the almost invisible levels of terraces. Thousands of square miles of Italy have been lifted in human hands, piled and laid back in tiny little flats, held up by the drystone walls, whose stones came from the lifted earth. It is a work of many, many centuries. It is the gentle sensitive sculpture of all the landscape. And it is the achieving of the peculiar Italian beauty which is so exquisitely natural, because man, feeling his way sensitively to the fruitfulness of the earth, has moulded the earth to his necessity without violating it.

Essay entitled "Flowery Tuscany" from *Phoenix*
D. H. LAWRENCE


Ten thousand writers have attempted to describe Florence, but one of the best, as usual, is Stendhal. So we had better let him continue his long say, as though listening to a monologue by a brilliant conversationalist.


### *Florence*

The day before yesterday, as I descended upon Florence from the high ridges of the Apennines, my heart was leaping wildly within me. What utterly childish excitement! At long last, at a sudden bend in the road, my gaze plunged downward into the heart of the plain, and there, in the far distance, like some darkling mass, I could distinguish the sombre pile of Santa Maria del Fiore with its famous Dome, the masterpiece of Brunelleschi.

"Behold the home of Dante, of Michelangelo, of Leonardo da Vinci", I mused within my heart. "Behold then this noble city, the Queen of mediaeval Europe! Here, within these walls, the civilisation of mankind was born anew; here it was that Lorenzo de' Medici so brilliantly sustained the part of Kingship, and established a Court at which, for the first time since the reign of Augustus, military prowess was reduced to a secondary role." As the minutes passed, so these memories came crowding and jostling one against the

65

other within my soul, and soon I found myself grown incapable of rational thought, but rather surrendered to the sweet turbulence of fancy, as in the presence of some beloved object. Upon approaching the *San-Gallo* gate, with its unbeautiful Triumphal Arch, I could gladly have embraced the first inhabitants of Florence whom I encountered.

At the risk of losing all that multitude of personal belongings which a man accumulates about him on his travels, immediately the ceremony of the *passport* had, with fitting ritual, been observed, I abandoned my conveyance. So often had I studied views of Florence, that I was familiar with the city before I ever set foot within its walls; I found that I could thread my way through the streets without a guide. Turning to the left, I passed before a bookseller's shop, where I bought a couple of descriptive surveys of the town (*guide*). Twice only was I forced to enquire my way of passers-by, who answered me with a politeness which was wholly French and with a most singular accent.

✵✵✵✵✵✵

All the live-long day, I roamed about in a sort of melancholy, historical abstraction. My first excursion led me to the church of *Santa Maria del Carmine*, which contains the Masaccio frescoes; after which, feeling myself ill-disposed properly to appreciate the oil-paintings of the *Palazzo Pitti* or of the *Uffizi*, I decided rather to visit the tombs of the Medici at *San Lorenzo*, together with the *Michelangelo Chapel*, so called on account of the sculptures executed by this great man. Emerging from *San Lorenzo*, I began to wander aimlessly about the streets, contemplating, from the wordless depths of my own emotion (with my eyes wide-staring, and the power of speech utterly gone from me), those massive *palazzi*—those veritable fortresses and castle-keeps—built towards the year 1300 by the merchants of Florence. On the perimeter of that vast *piazza*, whose centre is occupied by the Cathedral of *Santa Maria del Fiore* (built in 1293), my glance lighted upon those long arcades, whose arches, with

66

their distant hint of gothic inspiration, rise to an elegant apex formed by the junction of two curves (similar to the upper section of the *fleur-de-lis* design which you may find engraved upon a five-franc piece). This style of design is found repeated above the door of every house in Florence; but a modern generation has built a wall to block the ancient arcades which used to encircle the immensity of that open space, in the midst of which, in splendid isolation, rises the mass of *Santa Maria del Fiore*.

I experienced a great joy for knowing no one, for having no fear of being forced to make conversation. The power of this mediaeval architecture took undisputed possession of all my faculties; I could believe that *Dante* was the companion of my steps. Today, since waking, I doubt whether so many as a dozen thoughts have crossed my mind for which I might not find a ready formulation in the lines of this great poet. I feel ashamed of these observations, which will surely earn me the reputation of an *egoist*.

As it is only too plain from the solid structure of these *palazzi*, put together out of great, rude blocks of stone left rough and rugged on the side which affronts the street, *danger* has all too often stalked the streets of Florence. Yet it is precisely the absence of danger in our own thoroughfares which makes us all so insignificant. I have just returned from spending a whole hour, alone and motionless, in the centre of the dark little courtyard of the *palazzo* erected in the *via Larga* by that Cosimo de' Medici, whom fools revere as the *Father of his Country*. The fewer efforts this architecture makes to imitate a Grecian temple—or in other words, the more directly it echoes the character of the men who built it, and their needs—the more I find it fascinating. However, in order to preserve this sombre illusion which, throughout the day, has peopled my fancy with such figures as Castruccio Castracani, Uguccione della Fagiola, etc., as though I might come upon them face to face at the corner of each street, I must resolutely avert my gaze, lest it fall upon the featureless, insignificant creatures who throng the streets today—those sublime streets still redolent of the passionate energies of the Middle Ages! For alas! the

67

present-day citizen of Florence is ignorant of the very semblance of passion. Even his avarice is not a passion; it is nothing but a convention—one among many—resulting from a marriage between intense vanity and extreme poverty.

Florence, whose thoroughfares are paved with massive blocks of white granite, irregular in shape, is of a cleanliness rarely encountered elsewhere; her streets are perfumed with a curious and characteristic odour. With the unique exception of one or two townships in the Low Countries, Florence bids fair to be acclaimed the cleanest city in the universe. Her graeco-gothic architecture has all the clean finish and the consummate artistry of a perfect miniature. Happily for the tangible beauty of Florence, her citizens, at the same instant when they forfeited their liberty, did likewise forfeit the *energy* which inspires the building of such massive structures. Consequently, those shameful façades in the style of *Piermarini* are nowhere found to shock the eye of the beholder; nor does anything disturb the exquisite harmony of these streets, instinct with the *Ideal Beauty* of the Middle Ages. There are a score of odd corners in Florence—for instance, as you come down from the *Ponte della Trinità* to pass before the *Palazzo Strozzi*—where the traveller may well believe himself to be living in the year 1500.

Yet, despite the rare beauty of these countless streets, so richly steeped in grandeur and in melancholy, there is nothing which bears comparison to the *Palazzo Vecchio*. This fortress, built in 1298 by the freely-offered contributions of the merchant guilds, surges upwards, with its brick-work battlements and its fantastically towering walls, not in some solitary and deserted spot, but in the very centre of the finest *piazza* in Florence. Southward, it looks down upon Vasari's noble *Gallery*; northward, it is set off by an equestrian statue of one of the Medici; while in a cluster about its foot stand Michelangelo's *David* and Benvenuto Cellini's *Perseus*, together with the charming *Loggia dei Lanzi* —in a word, all the artistic masterpieces of Florence and all the activity of her civilisation. By a fortunate circumstance, this *piazza* has grown to be the *boulevard de Gand* of the city, the constant thoroughfare for all and sundry. What monument of Grecian architecture could tell so many tales of men and deeds as this grim mediaeval fortress, rough-hewn, implacable and energetic as the century which gave it birth? "Up there", observed my *cicerone*, "from that high window on the northern face, they hanged Archbishop Pazzi in all his solemn pontifical attire."

In Florence, the *Palazzo Vecchio*—this stark, contrasting incarnation of the stern realities of mediaeval times set square amid the artistic glories of the past and the insignificant throng of modern *marchesini*—creates an impression of unparalleled grandeur and truth. Here, for the instruction of the philosophic mind, stand the masterpieces of those arts, whose genius was fired by the violence of passion and bore fruit, only to wither in a later century and fade, becoming petty, insignificant and misshapen when the tempest of desire ceased to swell the sails by which alone that frail craft, the human soul, so important when passion falters and evaporates, leaving it bereft alike of vice and virtue, is driven across the stormy seas of life.

This evening, seated on a cane chair in front of the coffee house in the centre of the great *piazza* facing the *Palazzo Vecchio*, neither the crowd nor the cold—the one as inconsiderable as the other—could prevent my eye from beholding the whole tapestry of incident which had been unfolded upon this same *piazza*. Here, on these very stones, Florence had risen a score of times in the name of *liberty*, while blood had flowed in the cause of an unworkable constitution. And now the rising moon, by imperceptible degrees, began to print the massive shadow of the *Palazzo Vecchio* upon the scoured flagstones of the *piazza*, and to lend her magic touch of mystery to the colonnades of the *Uffizi*, beneath whose arches gleamed the lights of houses, distant beyond the Arno.

STENDHAL *Rome, Naples and Florence*

I have not been in Florence as much as in Rome or Venice, or even several other Italian cities. I spent a time there as a very young man in a lodging-house in Piazza del Carmine across the Arno. The lodging-house was kept by a couple of flaccid sisters who were always being ill. The only other lodger was a student from Florence university who used to return to his room at meal-times where he ate alone. At each of his meals he drank a bottle of beer and after this he would sing to himself in a penetrating tenor voice traditional Italian folk-songs for about an hour. Almost as though the illness of the two sisters was contagious I caught a fever and was kept in bed. The sisters ascribed this fever to eating ices, drinking iced water, or getting sunstroke. They argued a lot about these alternative explanations. But in due course, after many warnings, I was allowed to recover and visit the glories of the city, some of which are ascribed in the following pages.

Since those days Florence has become crowded with motor-cars, German, British, French, and the streets are full of tourists being guided round. Being a guide in Italy seems to be no unpleasant métier, though at times guides embroider on history and, in the case of Florence, interpret the great quarrel between the Dominican friar Savonarola and the Borgia Pope, Alexander VI, which led to the solemn trial, strangling and burning of that fierce yet holy and yet again puritan man of the Church, according to their political and religious opinions. On solemn occasions the Florentines produce spectacles of pageantry based on their enormous traditions which, if not so vast as those of the Vatican, seem to me lighter and more artistic. Such occasions, with the trumpeters in costumes who seem to have walked out of medieval paintings, have as centrepiece the most extraordinary mayor in the world. His name is La Pira. He is a tiny Sicilian who gives all his money to the poor and lives with the austerity of a monk. He makes speeches about social justice and peace and the necessity of imitating Jesus Christ with quotations from Karl Marx, St Thomas Aquinas and the Gospels—and when he gets going he has a brilliant smile and does not stop easily. He has entertained Cardinals and Communist leaders, and leaders of all races, pink, yellow and black.

A hundred years ago Florence had a huge foreign colony—and of foreign residents the English were by far the most numerous and the richest (Americans in those days were fewer). The arrivals of English families, with their carriages and postilions and incredible nannies brewing tea and righteousness, were a curious spectacle. Of English poets who lived in Florence, Walter Savage Landor was the most constant. But the Brownings played their part.

## Booksellers

I found this book,
Gave a *lira* for it, eightpence English just,
(Mark the predestination!) when a Hand,
Always above my shoulder, pushed me once,
One day still fierce 'mid many a day struck calm,
Across a Square in Florence, crammed with booths.
Buzzing and blaze, noontide and market-time;
Towards Baccio's marble,—ay, the basement-ledge
O' the pedestal where sits and menaces
John of the Black Bands with the upright spear,
'Twixt palace and church,—Riccardi where they lived,
His race, and San Lorenzo where they lie.
This book,—precisely on that palace-step
Which, meant for lounging knaves o' the Medici,
Now serves re-venders to display their ware,—
'Mongst odds and ends of ravage, picture-frames
White through the worn gilt, mirror-sconces chipped,
Bronze angel-heads once knobs attached to chests,
(Handled when ancient dames chose forth brocade)
Modern chalk drawings, studies from the nude,
Samples of stone, jet, breccia, porphyry
Polished and rough, sundry amazing busts
In baked earth (broken, Providence be praised!)
A wreck of tapestry, proudly-purposed web
When reds and blues were indeed red and blue,
Now offered as a mat to save bare feet
(Since carpets constitute a cruel cost)
Treading the chill scagliola bedward: then
A pile of brown-etched prints, two *crazie* each,
Stopped by a conch a-top from fluttering forth
—Sowing the Square with works of one and the same
Master, the imaginative Sienese
Great in the scenic backgrounds—(name and fame
None of you know, nor does he fare the worse):
From these . . . Oh, with a Leonard going cheap
If it should prove, as promised, that Joconde
Whereof a copy contents the Louvre!—these

71

I picked this book from. Five compeers in flank
Stood left and right of it as tempting more—
A dog'-eared Spicilegium, the fond tale
O' the Frail One of the Flower, by young Dumas,
Vulgarised Horace for the use of schools,
The Life, Death, Miracles of Saint Somebody,
Saint Somebody Else, his Miracles, Death and Life—
With this, one glance at the lettered back of which,
And "Stall!" cried I: a *lira* made it mine.

ROBERT BROWNING The Ring and the Book

The original inhabitants of Tuscany were the Etruscans—
whose power stretched as far south as Rome. It is worth going to
see the paintings in Etruscan tombs at Tarquinia and elsewhere.
The Etruscans seem to have had vivid dreams of immortality and
their ideas about demons were very like those Dante had when
he wrote his Inferno. What connection there is is anyone's guess.

## *Who Were the Etruscans?*

The Etruscans are one of the "mystery peoples" of
antiquity, perhaps less mysterious now than they were fifty
or sixty years ago, thanks to archaeological research, a lost
civilisation belonging to that shadowy epoch of proto-
history which in Italy precedes the Roman. So much that
might have survived has perished through the Vandalism,
ignorance and fanaticism of mankind. Athenaeus mentions
a lost Greek treatise on the Tyrrhenians (Etruscans); the
Roman Emperor, Claudius, wrote a (lost) history of them;
vague misunderstood traditions are recorded in the first
two books of Livy. According to Herodotus (and "modern
scholarship", unless it has changed again) the Etruscans
came from Asia Minor and settled on the coast of Italy
(about 800 B.C.) and gradually occupied much of the peninsula until they were destroyed by the Romans, those
Prussians of the ancient world. What is left of Etruscan art,

especially the early tomb-paintings, shows a people who enjoyed life, and hence were called "immoral" by the Romans who stole their country. Already the Etruscans had evolved beyond that state of society where the sexes are at war, to one of cheerful companionship. Their language is still not understood, and they left no literature; or if they did, it was destroyed. Their affinities were with pre-classical Greece, but also with Minoan Crete, Assyria and Egypt. They were half-Oriental people living in the West, good sailors, great engineers, allies of the Carthaginians, sexually uninhibited, dancers and flute-players, banqueters and artists. Unfortunately, almost all that is certainly known or reasonably inferred about the Etruscans comes to us by the gloomy channel of tombs, tomb-decoration and tomb-furniture.

RICHARD ALDINGTON

Introduction to *Etruscan Places* by D. H. LAWRENCE

### Clue to the Etruscans

The clue to the Etruscan life was the Lucumo, the religious prince. Beyond him were the priests and warriors. Then came the people and the slaves. People and warriors and slaves did not think about religion. There would soon have been no religion left. They felt the symbols and danced the sacred dances. For they were always kept *in touch*, physically, with the mysteries. The "touch" went from the Lucumo down to the merest slave. The blood-stream was unbroken. But "knowing" belonged to the high-born, the pure-bred.

So, in the tombs we find only the simple, uninitiated vision of the people. There is none of the priest-work of Egypt. The symbols are to the artist just wonder-forms, pregnant with emotion and good for decoration. It is so all the way through Etruscan art. The artists evidently were of the people, artisans. Presumably they were of the old Italic stock, and understood nothing of the religion in its intricate form, as it had come in from the East: though doubtless the crude principles of the official religion were the same as those of the primitive religion of the aborigines. The same crude principles ran through the religions of all the barbaric world of that time, Druid or Teutonic or Celtic. But the newcomers in Etruria held secret the science and philosophy of their religion, and gave the people the symbols and the ritual, leaving the artists free to use the symbols as they would; which shows that there was no priest-rule.

Later, when scepticism came over all the civilised world, as it did after Socrates, the Etruscan religion began to die, Greeks and Greek rationalism flooded in, and Greek stories more or less took the place of the old Etruscan symbolic thought. Then again the Etruscan artists, uneducated, used the Greek stories as they had used the Etruscan symbols, quite freely making them over again just to please themselves.

But one radical thing the Etruscan people never forgot, because it was in their blood as well as in the blood of their masters: and that was the mystery of the journey out of life, and into death; the death-journey, and the sojourn in the after-life. The wonder of their soul continued to play round the mystery of this journey and this sojourn.

In the tombs we see it; throes of wonder and vivid feeling throbbing over death. Man moves naked and glowing through the universe. Then comes death: he dives into the sea, he departs into the underworld.

D. H. LAWRENCE Etruscan Places

But the Etruscan civilisation collapsed with the Celtic invasions of Italy several centuries B.C. and was absorbed into the Greco-Roman life. Here is an effort to reconstruct Roman country life in the nearby Lunigiana in the second century A.D.

## A Roman House

The traveller, descending from the slopes of Luna, even as he got his first view of the *Port-of-Venus*, would pause by the way, to read the face, as it were, of so beautiful a dwelling-place, lying away from the white road, at the point where it began to decline somewhat steeply to the marsh-land below. The building of pale red and yellow marble, mellowed by age, which he saw beyond the gates, was indeed but the exquisite fragment of a once large and sumptuous villa. Two centuries of the play of the sea wind were in the velvet of the mosses which lay along its inaccessible ledges and angles. Here and there the marble plates had slipped from their places, where the delicate weeds had forced their way. The graceful wildness which prevailed in garden and farm gave place to a singular nicety about the actual habitation, and a still more scrupulous sweetness and order reigned within. The old Roman architects seem to have well understood the decorative value of the floor—the real economy there was, in the production of rich interior effect, of a somewhat lavish expenditure upon the surface they trod on. The pavement of the hall had lost something of its evenness; but, though a little rough to the foot, polished and cared for like a piece of silver, looked, as mosaic-work is apt to do, its best in old age. Most noticeable among the ancestral masks, each in its little cedar chest below the cornice, was that of the wasteful but elegant Marcellus, with the quaint resemblance in its yellow waxen features to Marius, just then so full of animation and country colour. A chamber, curved ingeni-ously into oval form, which he had added to the mansion, still contained his collection of works of art; above all, that head of Medusa, for which the villa was famous. The spoilers of one of the old Greek towns on the coast had flung away or lost the thing, as it seemed, in some rapid flight across the river below, from the sands of which it was drawn up in a fisherman's net, with the fine golden *laminae* still clinging here and there to the bronze. It was Marcellus also who had contrived the prospect-tower of two storeys with the white pigeon-house above, so characteristic of the place. The little glazed windows in the uppermost chamber framed each its dainty landscape—the pallid crags of Carrara, like wildly twisted snow-drifts above the purple heath; the distant harbour with its freight of white marble going to sea; the lighthouse temple of *Venus Speciosa* on its dark headland, amid the long-drawn curves of white breakers. Even on summer nights the air there had always a motion in it, and drove the scent of the new-mown hay along all the passages of the house.

WALTER PATER Marius the Epicurean

Country people in Tuscany have a sharp, almost derisive air.


## *Country Folk in Tuscany*

Seated without the Leghorn Gate, where I am wont to idle away many a long hour, it has been my pastime to observe the peasant women, and to note the rare degree of beauty in their eyes; yet there is no trace in their expression of that dreamy sensuality, no sign of that *susceptibility to passion* which characterises the women of Lombardy. Here, in Tuscany, the one quality which you may never discover is that strange *capacity for exaltation*; instead, by way of compensation, you may discern no lack of mental alertness, of pride, of rational intelligence, together with an elusive hint of provocative malice. I know of nothing so captivating as the glance of these handsome peasant-women, beneath their delicious head-dress with its black plume nodding and curtseying above their mannish hats. Yet I sense in such sharp and glittering eyes a deeper power of criticism than of adoration. I can never mistake that rational, speculative glint, nor discern in their look the potential *irrationality* of love. These madonna-eyes flash with the mocking light of battle rather than with the softer fires of passion.

The country-folk of Tuscany, as I will most readily believe, form the oddest and the wittiest peasantry in Italy. They may well be accounted, within the bounds of their condition, the most civilised race in all the world. They look upon religion much rather as a social convention, whose ill-observance would constitute *a breach of good manners*, than as a *Faith*; and Hell holds few terrors for such as they.

STENDHAL *Rome, Naples and Florence*

All Tuscany and Umbria is dotted with little towns on hilltops or the sides of hills, often hemmed in by medieval walls. They are still as they were when they formed backgrounds to the frescoes and paintings of sacred subjects by the early masters. Assisi, birthplace of St Francis, about whom I shall have more to say, is one of these towns.

## *Assisi*

I did have to take one hot walk that summer. Gertrude Stein insisted that no one could go to Assisi except on foot. She has three favourite saints, Saint Ignatius Loyola, Saint Theresa of Avila and Saint Francis. I alas have only one favourite saint, Saint Anthony of Padua, because it is he who finds lost objects and as Gertrude Stein's elder brother once said of me, if I were a general I would never lose a battle, I would only mislay it. Saint Anthony helps me find it. I always put a considerable sum in his box in every church I visit. At first Gertrude Stein objected to this extravagance but now she realises its necessity and if I am not with her she remembers Saint Anthony for me.

It was a very hot Italian day and we started as usual about noon, that being Gertrude Stein's favourite walking hour, because it was hottest and beside presumably Saint Francis had walked it then the oftenest as he had walked it at all hours. We started from Perugia across the hot valley. I gradually undressed, in those days one wore many more clothes than one does now, I even, which was most unconventional in those days, took off my stockings, but even so dropped a few tears before we arrived and we did arrive. Gertrude Stein was very fond of Assisi for two reasons, because of Saint Francis and the beauty of his city and because the old women used to lead instead of a goat a little

77

pig up and down the hills of Assisi. The little black pig was always decorated with a red ribbon. Gertrude Stein had always liked little pigs and she always said that in her old age she expected to wander up and down the hills of Assisi with a little black pig. . . .

GERTRUDE STEIN
*The Autobiography of Alice B. Toklas*

# Italian Religion

ENGLISH-SPEAKING visitors to Italy seem to find it hard to understand Italian religion—which they easily think of as pagan, superstitious and even blasphemous. The Italians are equally mystified by the British and Americans. They are unable to understand Puritanism and they suspect hypocrisy. Here is one version of the difference in an imaginary conversation by Madame de Staël, herself a Swiss Protestant. Corinne, the Roman girl is talking to the Scottish nobleman, Oswald, who is in love with her.

## *Catholicism and Protestantism*

"The difference between our religions, my dear Oswald," Corinne went on, "is the real cause of the secret blame you can't conceal from me. Your religion is strict and serious; ours is lively and tender. It is commonly supposed that Catholicism is stricter than Protestantism, and that may well be true in countries where there has been a struggle between the two religions; but in Italy we have no religious controversies whereas you in England have undergone many; as a result of this difference, in Italy Catholicism has developed a gentle, indulgent character, whereas, so as to destroy Catholicism in England, the Reformation armed itself with extreme severity both in principles and morals. Our religion, like that of the ancient world, gives life to the arts, inspires poets, and, so to speak, participates in all the pleasures of our life; whereas yours, which was set up in a country where reason was even more preponderant than imagination, took on a character of moral austerity which

79

it will never stray from. Our religion speaks in the name of love; yours in the name of duty. Our principles are liberal, though our dogmas are absolute; nevertheless in practice our despotic orthodoxy adapts itself to individual circumstances; and your religious freedom demands that all your laws should be respected without any exception. True, our Catholicism imposes severe penances on those who have taken up the monastic state; this state, which is freely chosen, is a mysterious link between man and the Divine; but the religion of people in the world, in Italy, is a habitual source of touching emotions. The principal virtues of this religion are love, hope and faith; and all these virtues herald and create happiness. So our priests, far from at any time forbidding us the pure sentiment of joy, tell us that this sentiment expresses our gratitude for the Creator's gifts. What they demand of us is to observe practices that prove our respect for our religion and our desire to please God; these consist in charity for the unfortunate and repentance for our weaknesses. But they never refuse to absolve us when we ask them to do so ardently; and here more than elsewhere the attachments of the heart inspire an indulgent pity. Didn't Jesus Christ say to Mary Magdalen: 'She will be forgiven much because she loved much'? These words were said beneath heavens as beautiful as ours: and the same heavens implore for us the mercy of the Divine Being."

MADAME DE STAËL Corinne

The central ceremony in Italy, as in all Catholic countries, is the Mass.

## The Mass

The Mass, indeed, would appear to have been said continuously from the Apostolic age. Its details, as one by one they become visible in later history, have already the character of what is ancient and venerable. "We are very old, and ye are young!" they seem to protest, to those who

*The ancient city of Lucca*

*Even the little walled city of San Gimignano was a re-
public in the Middle Ages, and the towers were fortresses*

fail to understand them. Ritual, in fact, like all other elements of religion, must grow and cannot be made—grow by the same law of development which prevails everywhere else, in the moral as in the physical world. As regards this special phase of the religious life, however, such development seems to have been unusually rapid in the subterranean age which preceded Constantine; and in the very first days of the final triumphs of the church the Mass emerges to general view already substantially complete. "Wisdom" was dealing, as with the dust of creeds and philosophies, so also with the dust of outworn religious usage, like the very spirit of life itself, organising soul and body out of the lime and clay of the earth. In a generous eclecticism, within the bounds of her liberty, and as by some providential power within her, she gathers and serviceably adopts, as in other matters so in ritual, one thing here, another there, from various sources—Gnostic, Jewish, Pagan—to adorn and beautify the greatest act of worship the world has seen. It was thus the liturgy of the church came to be—full of consolations for the human soul, and destined, surely! one day under, the sanction of so many ages of human experience, to take exclusive possession of the religious consciousness.

> TANTUM ERGO SACRAMENTUM
> VENEREMUR CERNUI:
> ET ANTIQUUM DOCUMENTUM
> NOVO CEDAT RITUI.
>
> WALTER PATER *Marius the Epicurean*

In the Italian tradition there is a vein of deep simple piety.

### Religion of a Peasant

But before stretching himself out on this bed which Providence had provided for him, he knelt down to thank God for this blessing and for all the help which he had had from Him during that terrible day. Then he said his usual prayers, asking God's pardon, moreover, for not having

81

said them the night before—for having—to use his own
words—gone to bed like a dog or worse.—And that was
why . . . !—he added to himself then, leaning his hands on
the straw and stretching out from kneeling to lying—and
that was why I had that fine awakening this morning.—
Then he gathered up all the straw left around him and
arranged it over himself, making the best blanket he could
to temper the cold, which even in there made itself quite
keenly felt, and curled himself up underneath it, intending
to have a really good sleep, which he felt he had earned over
and over again.

ALESSANDRO MANZONI The Betrothed<br>Trans. Archibald Colquhoun

Italy has produced more saints than any other country. But
the most typical and most loved of all Italian saints is St Francis
of Assisi. His early followers seemed to re-live the Sermon on the
Mount with childlike confidence.

### *Friar Giles, Beatnik*

Friar Giles went, by leave of St Francis, to visit the Holy
Sepulchre of Christ, and came to the port of Brindisi, and
there stayed over many days, for there was no ship ready.
And Friar Giles, desiring to live by his labour, begged a
pitcher, and filling it with water, went about the city crying,
"Who lacks water?" And for his toil he received bread and
things needful for the life of the body, both for himself and
for his companion. And then he crossed the seas, and visited
the Holy Sepulchre of Christ, and the other holy places, with
great devotion. And journeying back, he abode many days
in the city of Ancona; and forasmuch as he was wont to
live by the labour of his hands, he made baskets of rushes
and sold them, not for money, but for bread for himself
and for his companion; and he carried the dead to burial
for the aforesaid price. And when these things failed him, he
returned to the table of Jesus Christ, asking alms from door

to door. And thus, with much toil and poverty, he came back to St Mary of the Angels. . . .

Friar Giles, being on a time in the friary in Rome, was minded to live by bodily toil, even as he was ever wont to do since he entered the Order, and he wrought in this wise: Betimes, in the morning, he heard mass with much devotion, then he went to the wood that was eight miles distant from Rome and carried a faggot of wood back on his shoulders, and sold it for bread, or aught else to eat. One time, among others, when he was returning with a load of wood, a woman asked to buy it; and being agreed on the price, he carried it to her house. The woman, notwithstanding the bargain, gave him much more than she had promised, for she saw he was a religious. Saith Friar Giles, "Good woman, I would not that the sin of avarice overcome me, therefore I will not take a greater price than I bargained with thee". And not only would he take no more, but he took only the half price agreed upon, and went his way; wherefore that woman conceived a very great devotion for him. Friar Giles did any honest work for hire, and always gave heed to holy honesty; he gave a hand to gather olives and to tread the wine-press for the peasants. Standing on a day in the market-place, a certain man sought hands to beat down his walnuts, and begged one to beat them down for him, at a price; but he made excuse, saying it was very far away, and the trees were very hard to climb. Saith Friar Giles, "Friend, an thou wilt give me part of the walnuts I will come with thee and beat them down." The bargain made, he went his way, and, first making the sign of the holy cross, he climbed up to beat a tall walnut tree with great fear. And after he had beaten the branches thereof so many walnuts were due to him for his share that he could not carry them away in his lap. Wherefore he took off his habit and bound up the sleeves and the cowl, and made a sack thereof, and having filled this his habit with walnuts, he lifted it on to his shoulder and carried the walnuts to Rome; and he gave all to the poor, with great joy, for love of God. When the corn was cut, Friar Giles went with the other poor folk to glean some ears; and if any one offered him a handful of corn he answered, "Brother, I have no granary wherein to store it." And the ears of wheat he gleaned he gave away, more often than not, for love of God. Seldom did Friar Giles work the whole day through, for he always bargained to have some space of time to say the canonical hours and not fail in his mental prayers. Once on a time Friar Giles went to the fountain of San Sisto to draw water for the monks, and a man asked him for a drink. Friar Giles answered, "And how shall I carry this vessel half filled to the monks?" And this man angrily spake many words of contumely and abuse to Friar Giles: and Friar Giles returned to the monks grieving much. Begging a large vessel anon he returned to the said fountain for water, and finding that man again, said to him, "My friend, take and drink as much as thy soul desireth, and be not angry, for methinks 'tis a base thing to take water that hath been drunk of, to those holy monks." He, pricked and constrained by the charity and humility of Friar Giles, confessed his fault, and from that hour forth held him in great veneration.

ANON. *The Little Flowers of St Francis*

All travellers to Italy want to visit San Gimignano, the medieval fortress town with its towers rising above it like upright hair, and above all Siena. Siena is the largest of the almost completely medieval cities. It is here that the best Italian is claimed to be spoken, and the Siennese still remember the days when they were the great rivals of Florence in political power. They also had their own Siennese school of painting which remained Gothic and stiff after the Florentines had moved over to the more flowing and humanistic manner of the Renaissance. The most popular spectacle in Siena is known as the Palio. This consists of a horse race round the central square of the city—called the Campo—in which the riders wear medieval costumes. Siena is divided into districts known as *contrade*, and each *contrada* produces its best rider who of course wears its colours. Siena also produced one of the most attractive of saints. This was the Franciscan, Bernardino. He preached to the people spontaneously and what he said was taken down by adoring scribes. He was a great Tuscan wit as well as a saint.

## Franciscan Religion: A Wrong Vocation

I got the idea that I wanted to live on grass and water, and decided to go and stay in a wood and began saying to myself: What are you to do in a wood? What are you to eat? And I said to myself, by way of answer: All right, what did the Holy Fathers do? I'll eat grass when I'm hungry and I'll drink water when I'm thirsty. And that's what I thought of doing; and so as to live God's way I also decided to buy a Bible. . . . And I bought the Bible and went to buy some leather so that the water shouldn't get in and wet the Bible. And with this in mind I went to look for somewhere to perch and made up my mind to go and look around as far as Massa; and when I was in the valley of the Boccheggiano, I wandered about looking at one little hill after another and saying to myself: Ho, this will be the good life, here. No, it would be even better there. But to cut a story short I went back to Siena and decided to begin trying out the sort of life I wanted to lead. So I went outside the gate to Follonica and began gathering a salad of thistles and other rough herbs, and I had neither bread not salt nor oil; and I said: Let's begin this time by washing and peeling it, then the next time we'll only peel it without any washing; and when we've got more used to it we'll eat it without cleaning it, and then we'll eat it without pulling it out of the ground. And in the name of the Blessed Jesus I began with a mouthful of thistle and putting it in my mouth I began to chew it. I chewed and chewed but it wouldn't go down. As I couldn't swallow it I said, let's begin by drinking a gulp of water. But lo. The water went down and the thistle remained in my mouth. All told, I drank a number of gulps of water for one mouthful of thistle, and I couldn't swallow it. Do you get my point? One mouthful of thistle took away all temptation; for I know for certain that this was temptation. What came later wasn't temptation, but election. Oh, what a lot of weighing up ought to go on before anyone follows the dictates of their will that often turn out to be very bad though they look very good. That's why Saint Bernard said: *Non semper credendum est bonae voluntati.* No, you just mustn't always go believing in the goodness of your will. But—what about the saints of old, as in the times of the Holy Fathers, what did they do? Well, they lived on grass. I answer you. *Distingue tempora; et concordabis scripturas.* Distinguish the times. Don't you realise the things the saints could do, and you couldn't. Or what Saint Francis did, going on a fast for forty days, and not eating a single thing. He could do this, I couldn't. And I tell you I don't want to do it; and I wouldn't want God to give me the taste for it. It's the same I tell you about Saint Peter; of course you know how he went on the water, just as you go on the ground. But you wouldn't catch me trying that! So this leads to saying that you mustn't want to do what you think you aren't capable of doing; for if you wanted to do it, it would kill you. Just think that if a farmer put a weight on his ass bigger than he could carry, he'd skin him alive; if he wants to put it on him, he has to put it on the place where he's strong enough. If he put it on his neck, he'd skin him alive; and it would be just the same if he put it on his tail. But if he puts it on his middle, he can carry it.

SAN BERNARDINO OF SIENA *Sermons*


If Giotto expressed Franciscan spirituality in his frescoes at Assisi or Padua, Fra Angelico did the same for the Dominicans, the other great religious order of the Middle Ages.


### Fra Angelico's Character

Fra Giovanni Angelico da Fiesole was no less eminent as a painter and a miniaturist than as an ecclesiastic and on each account deserves to be honourably remembered. He might have made a most comfortable living in the world, having means of his own and the ability to earn as much as he liked by his art. But he chose to enter the Order of Preaching Friars, the better to serve God and to seek his own salvation.

✳ ✳ ✳ ✳ ✳ ✳

86

And now the Pope, judging Fra Angelico to be, as indeed he was, a most holy, gentle, and modest soul, proposed to appoint him archbishop of Florence. But Fra Angelico begged to be excused, since he did not feel capable of ruling men. He suggested instead a man of the Order who was skilled in the art of governing others, a friend of the poor, and one who feared God. The Pope granted him the favour, and thus was Fra Antonio of the Order of Friars-Preachers made archbishop of Florence. This prelate was most illustrious in learning and sanctity and fully deserved the canonisation bestowed upon him in our own day by Pope Adrian VI.

\* \* \* \* \* \*

So sublime a gift as that possessed by Fra Angelico should scarcely be conferred on any but a man of most holy life. When sacred subjects are attempted by persons of little faith, they often cause light thoughts to awaken in the beholder and are censured for this, even if they are able works of art. I would not seem to say that rude and inept things are therefore holy, and the beautiful and attractive are licentious, though this is a common error. By some people, feminine and youthful figures are instantly considered licentious. These people wrongfully condemn the sound judgment of the painter, who has made celestial beings so far superior to mere mortals in beauty as heaven is to earth. These critics betray the impurity of their own hearts, which do not aspire to the beauty and perfection of heaven but seek to discover evil. What are we to suppose these people do when they are exposed to living beauty, light manners, and seductive grace, and eyes that cannot but ravish? What then, if they are so troubled by a mere picture? I would not seem to approve of almost entirely nude figures in church. The painter must take into consideration the reserve due to the place, even though he desires to exhibit the extent of his ability.

Fra Giovanni was the most simple of men, and pious in every act of his life. It is told that when he was invited to breakfast with Pope Nicholas V, he scrupled to eat meat without permission of his prior. He disregarded all worldly things and was so much a friend of the poor in life that I believe his soul is now in heaven. He painted incessantly but would not think of doing anything that was not holy. He might have been rich but he did not care to be. On the contrary, he used to say that true wealth was contentment with little. He might have held a position of great authority, but he would not, saying that there was less danger of error in being ruled than in ruling. He declared that he sought no dignity and had no care but to escape hell and to draw near to paradise.

Fra Giovanni was kindly to all. He was moderate in all his habits and held himself apart from the snares of the world. He used to say that painters needed peace and freedom from anxiety, and that one who would do the work of Christ should belong to Christ. He was never seen to display anger, a thing which seems to me almost incredible. If he admonished his friends it was with a gentle smile. If anyone wanted a picture, he answered with the utmost cordiality that they must get permission of the prior and then he would surely do what they wanted. This father was a most modest, humble, and excellent man in both word and deed, and the saints that he painted so ably have more the air and expression of sanctity than have those of any other master.

VASARI *Lives of the Painters*

### God's in His Heaven . . .

Over this realm of feeling Fra Angelico was the first great master. "God's in his heaven—all's right with the world" he felt with an intensity which prevented him from perceiving evil anywhere. When he was obliged to portray it, his imagination failed him and he became a mere child; his hells are bogy-land; his martyrdoms are enacted by children solemnly playing at martyr and executioner; and he nearly spoils one of the most impressive scenes ever painted—the great "Crucifixion" at San Marco—with the

*Tuscany, land of hills and fertile fields and work*

The monks at Camaldoli in Tuscany live and die in contemplation and prayer. At meal times they listen to
readings from the Bible and the lives of the saints

*St Francis of Assisi loved the birds and the flowers and dis-
trusted fine architecture. But his followers had to raise
a monument to his memory—and have Giotto paint the frescoes*

*Genoa: emigrants set out and return, but they never forget their families and their household gods*

childish violence of St Jerome's tears. But upon the picturing of blitheness, of ecstatic confidence in God's loving care, he lavished all the resources of his art. Nor were they small. To a power of rendering tactile values, to a sense for the significant in composition, inferior, it is true, to Giotto's, but superior to the qualifications of any intervening painter, Fra Angelico added the charm of great facial beauty, the interest of vivid expression, the attraction of delicate colour. What in the whole realm of art more rejuvenating than Angelico's "Coronation"—the happiness on all the faces, the flower-like grace of line and colour, the childlike simplicity yet unqualifiable beauty of the composition? And all this in tactile values which compel us to grant the reality of the scene, although in a world where real people are standing, sitting, and kneeling we know not, and care not, on what. It is true, the significance of the event represented is scarcely touched upon, but then how well Angelico communicates the feeling with which it inspired him! Yet simple though he was as a person, simple and one-sided as was his message, as a product he was singularly complex. He was the typical painter of the transition from Medieval to Renaissance. The sources of his feeling are in the Middle Ages, but he *enjoys* his feelings in a way which is almost modern; and almost modern also are his means of expression. We are too apt to forget this transitional character of his, and, ranking him with the moderns, we count against him every awkwardness of action, and every lack of articulation in his figures. Yet both in action and in articulation he made great progress upon his precursors—so great that, but for Masaccio, who completely surpassed him, we should value him as an innovator. Moreover, he was not only the first Italian to paint a landscape that can be identified (a view of Lake Trasimene from Cortona), but the first to communicate a sense of the pleasantness of nature. How readily we feel the freshness and springtime and gaiety of his gardens in the frescoes of the "Annunciation" and the "Noli me tangere" at San Marco!

BERNHARD BERENSON
*The Italian Painters of the Renaissance*

89

But not all painter-friars were as austere as Fra Angelico.


### *Fra Filippo Lippi's Baby*

Fra Filippo lived for some months in Prato, painting for the whole surrounding district. With him was the Carmelite Fra Diamante, who had been his companion when a novice. He received a commission from the nuns of Santa Margherita to paint a picture for their high altar. He happened to see the daughter of Francesco Buti, a citizen of Florence, who had been sent to the convent either as novice or boarder. After one glance at Lucrezia (for that was her name), Filippo persuaded the nuns to let her sit for him for the figure of the Virgin he was painting for them. The result was that the painter fell madly in love and at last prevailed upon Lucrezia to escape with him on the day she had gone forth to do honour to the girdle of the Virgin, the venerated relic preserved at Prato and exhibited once a year. The nuns were deeply disgraced by this event. But Lucrezia, whether from fear or some other cause, would not return and remained with Filippo, to whom she bore a son who was also called Filippo and who eventually became a most famous painter like his father.

VASARI *Lives of the Painters*


As Robert Browning put it:

I am poor brother Lippo, by your leave!
You need not clap your torches to my face.
Zooks, what's to blame? You think you see a monk?
What, it's past midnight, and you go the rounds,
And here you catch me at an alley's end
Where sportive ladies leave their doors ajar?

But here is another aspect of Italian religion, equally popular. Benvenuto Cellini, the great Renaissance metal worker, lived anything but a pious life, as we shall see. But for all that he revered the power of the saints.

## Offering to Saint Lucy

Now one morning I was sharpening some chisels before beginning my work, when the finest splinter of steel flew into my right eye, entering the pupil so far that it could not be taken out by any means. I thought for certain I should lose the sight of that eye. At the end of several days I called in Maestro Raffaello de' Pilli, the surgeon. He brought with him two live pigeons. Then laying me down on my back on a table, with the knife he cut open a great vein in the birds' wings, so that the blood spurted out into my eye. This eased me at once; by two days the splinter was out, and I was at rest, with my eyesight better than before. The feast of St Lucy coming on in three days, I made a golden eye out of a French crown; and had it offered at the saint's shrine by one of my six nieces, the daughters of my sister Liperata. She was about ten years old; and I went with her to church to thank God and St Lucy. For some time I gave up working on the Narcissus, but I got on with my Perseus, though under the difficulties I have already spoken of; for I had a mind to finish it, and then to be off.

BENVENUTO CELLINI *Memoirs*

Stendhal, the Frenchman, could not resist passing rationalistic comments on the spontaneity of the religious feeling that he observed so brilliantly in the hero of his novel *The Charterhouse of Parma*, Fabrizio del Dongo, passionate lover and candidate for the Archbishopric.

## Fabrizio's Religion

On arriving in Bologna, Fabrizio, feeling extremely tired and not venturing, without a passport, to show his face at an inn, had gone into the huge church of San Petronio. He found there a delicious coolness; presently he felt quite revived. "Ungrateful wretch that I am," he said to himself suddenly, "I go into a church, simply to sit down, as it might be in a *caffè*!" He threw himself on his knees and thanked God effusively for the evident protection with which he had been surrounded ever since he had had the misfortune to kill Giletti. The danger which still made him shudder had been that of his being recognised in the police office at Casalmaggiore. "How," he asked himself, "did that clerk, whose eyes were so full of suspicion, who read my passport through at least three times, fail to notice that I am not five feet ten inches tall, that I am not thirty-eight years old, and that I am not strongly pitted by small-pox? What thanks I owe to Thee, O my God! And I have actually refrained until this moment from casting the nonentity that I am at Thy feet. My pride has chosen to believe that it was to a vain human prudence that I owed the good fortune of escaping the Spielberg, which was already opening to engulf me."

Fabrizio spent more than an hour in this state of extreme emotion, in the presence of the immense bounty of God. Lodovico approached, without his hearing him, and took his stand opposite him. Fabrizio, who had buried his face in his hands, raised his head, and his faithful servant could see the tears streaming down his cheeks.

"Come back in an hour," Fabrizio ordered him, somewhat harshly.

Lodovico forgave this tone in view of the speaker's piety. Fabrizio repeated several times the Seven Penitential Psalms, which he knew by heart; he stopped for a long time at the verses which had a bearing on his situation at the moment.

Fabrizio asked pardon of God for many things, but what is really remarkable is that it never entered his head to number among his faults the plan of becoming Archbishop simply because Conte Mosca was Prime Minister and felt that office and all the importance it implied to be suitable for the Duchessa's nephew. He had desired it without passion, it is true, but still he had thought of it exactly as one might think of being made a Minister or a General. It had never entered his thoughts that his conscience might be concerned in this project of the Duchessa. This is a remarkable characteristic of the religion which he owed to the instruction given him by the Jesuits of Milan. That religion *deprives one of the courage to think of unfamiliar things,* and especially forbids *personal examination,* as the most enormous of sins; it is a step towards Protestantism. To find out of what sins one is guilty, one must question one's priest, or read the list of sins, as it is to be found printed in the book entitled *Preparation for the Sacrament of Penance.* Fabrizio knew by heart the list of sins, rendered into the Latin tongue, which he had learned at the Ecclesiastical Academy of Naples. So, when going through that list, on coming to the article, *Murder,* he had most forcibly accused himself before God of having killed a man, but in defence of his own life. He had passed rapidly, and without paying them the slightest attention, over the various articles relating to the sin of *Simony* (the procuring of ecclesiastical dignities with money). If anyone had suggested to him that he should pay a hundred louis to become First Grand Vicar of the Archbishop of Parma, he would have rejected such an idea with horror; but, albeit he was not wanting in intelligence, nor above all in logic, it never once occurred to his mind that the employment on his behalf of Conte Mosca's influence was a form of Simony. This is where the Jesuitical education triumphs: it forms the habit of not paying attention to things that are clearer than daylight. A Frenchman, brought up among conflicting personal interests and in the prevailing irony of Paris might, without being deliberately unfair, have accused Fabrizio of hypocrisy at the very moment when our hero was opening his soul to God with the utmost sincerity and the most profound emotion.

STENDHAL *The Charterhouse of Parma*


Often, in a society in which religion plays so material a part, ecclesiastical preferment was—and still can be—a cause of conflict in families in which the woman, the mother, wins in the end.


## *The Making of a Canon*

The Count had a brother who in no way resembled him and was an honorary canon of the Cathedral at Portogruaro, the roundest, smoothest and most mellifluous canon in the whole diocese, a real man of peace who divided his time wisely between the breviary and the table without letting his greater predilection for the one or for the other be revealed. Monsignor Orlando was not begotten by milord his father with any idea of dedicating him to Mother Church; his baptismal name was witness for this. The genealogical tree of the Counts of Fratta had always boasted some military glory in every generation, and he had been destined to perpetuate the family tradition. But man proposes and God disposes; this time at least the great proverb was not wrong. The future General began his life by demonstrating an extraordinary affection for his wet-nurse, so that it was not possible to wean him before the age of two. Even at that time it was still uncertain whether the one word he could utter was "pap" or "papa".

When he was at last able to walk, they began putting wooden swords and cardboard helmets in his hands; but hardly had they done so before he escaped into the chapel to play with the sacristan's broom. As for trying to accustom him to real weapons, he showed from the first an instinctive revulsion against table knives and wanted at all costs to cut his meat up with a spoon. His father tried to vanquish this accursed repugnance by making him sit on the knee of one of his *buli* (feudal retainers); but the little Orlando was so terrified that they had to transfer him to the cook's lap lest he should die of fright. After the wet-nurse, the cook was his second love; it was not for nothing that he made clear his vocation. The Chancellor held that the captains of old time always ate so much that the little master would indeed in course of time become a famous captain.

The old Court was not reassured by these hopes, and sighed as his eyes wandered from the puffy and bewildered face of his second-born to the proud and hirsute moustachios of the old family portraits. He had dedicated the last powers of his generative faculties to the ambitious task of inscribing in the future annals of the family a Grand Master of the Order of Malta or an Admiral of the Most Serene Republic, and it galled him to have employed them merely

94

to have at his table the terrific appetite of a Captain of the Cernide (local militia). Therefore he redoubled his zeal to awaken and stir up the bellicose spirit of Orlando; but the effect did not justify his efforts. Orlando built little altars in every corner of the castle, sang Mass, high, low and ceremonial, with the sacristan's brats, and whenever he saw a musket flattened himself under one of the kitchen side-boards. Then they tried other means of persuasion, forbidding him to play in the sacristy and to sing vespers through his nose as he had heard the choirboys of the parish do. But his mother was scandalised by such violence and began, on her side, secretly to take up the defence of her son. Orlando found it much to his taste to act the part of a little martyr; and since his mother's sweetmeats amply consoled him for his father's rebuffs, the profession of a priest seemed to him more than ever preferable to that of a soldier. The cook and the house-servants sniffed around him an odour of sanctity and thenceforward he began to grow fat with contentment and to show an even more exaggerated devotion in order to maintain the adoration of the womenfolk. So that finally his august father, with his military ambitions, had against him the opinion of the whole family. Even the *buli*, who always supported the cook's party when their feudal master was out of hearing, deplored the sacrilege of obstinately trying to turn a St Louis from the true path. But the feudal master was obstinate and only after twelve years of vain assault decided to lift the siege and to put away in the storehouse of vanished dreams the future military laurels of Orlando. One fine morning Orlando was called with imposing solemnity before his father who, however much he outwardly assumed the authoritative frown of the absolute master, yet felt within him the vacillating and contrite feelings of a general about to capitulate.

"My son," he began, "the profession of arms is a noble profession."

"So I believe," replied the boy with a saintly expression, a little marred by a sly glance secretly directed towards his mother.

95

"You bear a proud name," continued the old Count, sighing, "Orlando, as you must have learnt from the poem of Ariosto which I have so much recommended you to study. . . ."

"I read the Offices of the Madonna," interrupted the boy, humbly.

"Excellent," continued the old man, adjusting the wig on his forehead, "but Ariosto is also worthy of being read. Orlando was a great paladin who liberated from the Moors the fair realm of France. And even more, if you have glanced through *Gerusalemme Liberata*, you would know that it was not with the Offices of the Madonna, but with great strokes of the sword and thrusts of the lance that the good Geoffrey wrested from the hands of the Saracens the Sepulchre of Christ."

"May God be praised," exclaimed the boy. "Then there remains nothing more to be done!"

"Nothing more, indeed!" burst out the old man. "Know then, wretched boy, that the infidels reconquered the Holy Land and that now, even as we are speaking, a Pasha of the Sultan governs Jerusalem to the shame of all Christendom!"

"I will pray the Good Lord that such shame should cease," put in Orlando.

"Prayers, indeed! It is deeds that are needed," shouted the old Count.

"Your pardon," interrupted the Countess, "but you surely do not pretend that our baby should carry out a crusade all by himself."

"Bah! He is no longer a baby," replied the Count. "He has just completed his twelfth year."

"Even had he completed his hundredth," went on the Countess, "it is certainly not necessary to fill his head with the conquest of Palestine."

"We shall never conquer it as long as we teach our children to play the woman with a rosary," exclaimed the old man, purple with anger.

"It only wanted that sort of blasphemy!" the Countess went on patiently. "Since the Good Lord has granted us a

*On the old Appian Way*

*The Spanish Steps (named after the old Spanish em-
bassy) and the church of Trinità dei Monti are a famous
example of the poem in stone that was papal Rome*

son who has the idea of being good, let us show ourselves grateful indeed by refusing to recognise his gifts!"

"Fine gifts, fine gifts!" muttered the Count, ". . . a gluttonous little saintling . . . half fox and half rabbit. . . ."

"At least he never said anything like that," added the lady. "All he said was that he would pray to God to grant that the places of His passion and His death return to the hands of the Christians. That is the best thing to do now, since the Christians of today are occupied in cutting one another's throats and the profession of soldier has become a mere school of cut-throats and butchers."

"Body of the Serenissima!" thundered the Count. "If Sparta had had mothers like you, Xerxes would have passed Thermopylae with three hundred hogsheads."

"Even had things been as you say, I should not have worried overmuch," replied the Countess.

"What!" roared the old man. "Have you reached the point of denying even the heroism of Leonidas and the virtue of the Spartan mothers?"

"Bah! Now we know where we are," the lady said quietly. "I know little enough of Leonidas and the Spartan mothers, though I have heard them mentioned only too often; furthermore, I am quite prepared to believe blindly that they were very fine fellows. But recall that we have summoned before us our son Orlando to throw some light on his true vocation and not to squabble in his presence about these rancid fairy-tales."

"Women, women! . . . Born to educate hens!" muttered the Count.

"Husband mine! I am a Badoera!" said the Countess, drawing herself up. "You will allow, I hope, that the hens in my family are not more numerous than the capons in yours!"

Orlando, who had been holding his sides for some time past, now broke into a laugh at this fine compliment of Madame his mother but was quelled instantly like a wet chicken at the severe glance she turned on him.

"You see," she went on, speaking to her husband, "we will end up by losing both goat and cabbages. Put a rein on

97

your caprices till God makes you understand He cannot be thwarted for nothing, and ask yourself instead, as becomes a good father of a family, about the soul of this boy."

The old impenitent bit his lip and turned to his son with an expression on his face so terrifying that the boy was scared out of his wits and ran to hide his head in his mother's lap.

"So," the old Count began, without looking at him, since he felt that if he did so his anger would rise again. "So, my son, you do not want to make your appearance on a fine horse, with trappings of gold and red velvet, with a long flaming sword in your hand and behind you six regiments of Slavs, all six feet high, who only wait an order from you to rush to their death on the Turkish scimitars?"

"I want to sing Masses, I do!" whimpered the boy from under his mother's apron.

The Count, hearing this whining voice half suffocated by the folds of the garment whence it issued, turned to see what was the matter, and seeing his son with his head wrapped up like a pheasant in its hide, could no longer control his anger.

"Go to the seminary then, bastard!" he shouted, rushing out of the room.

The little wretch began to sob and tear his hair and beat his head against his mother's lap, quite sure that he could not do himself any harm. But she took him in her arms and consoled him with caresses, saying:

"Yes, heart of mine, don't be afraid; we will make a priest of you. You will sing Mass. You are not made, indeed, to spill the blood of your brothers like Cain."

"Ee, ee, ee! I want to sing in the chair! I want to become a saint!" howled Orlando.

"Yes, yes . . . you will sing in the choir; we shall make a canon of you. You shall have your cloak and your fine red stockings. Don't cry, my treasure. These are trials which we must bear for the Good Lord's sake, to make ourselves more worthy of him," went on his mother.

The boy consoled himself with these promises, and therefore the Count Orlando, despite his baptismal name, and in opposition to his father's views, became Monsignor Orlando. But however much the Curia was disposed to favour the devout ambition of the Countess, none the less Orlando was no eagle, so that it took no less than twelve years in the seminary and another thirty as a postulant to help him to reach even the half of his aspirations; and the Count had the triumph, and the Countess the mortification, of dying many years before the red flakes began to snow down upon his head. None the less, it could not be said that our priest entirely wasted all this time of waiting. He acquired a respectable knowledge of the missal; and his shirt-front developed to such an extent that it would rival the softest and most elaborate of any of his colleagues.

IPPOLITO NIEVO The Castle of Fratta

Not all friars were as holy as St Francis. Boccaccio's *Decameron* contains many miniatures of false or hypocritical friars. One of the funniest concerns Fra Cipolla, who travelled round with a casket containing a feather. When he preached he said the feather was taken from the wing of St Michael the Archangel. But some young men tried to play a trick on him.

## Friar Cipolla, the Angel Gabriel and St Laurence

So the young men, having found the feather, took it out with great glee; and looking around for something to replace it, they espied in a corner of the room some pieces of coal, wherewith they filled the casket; which they then closed, and having set the room in order exactly as they had found it, they quitted it unperceived, and hied them merrily off with the feather, and posted themselves where they might hear what Fra Cipolla would say when he found the coals in its stead. Mass said, the simple folk that were in the church went home with the tidings that the feather of the Angel Gabriel was to be seen after none; and this goodman telling his neighbour, and that goodwife her gossip, by the time every one had breakfasted, the town could scarce hold

99

the multitude of men and women that flocked thither all agog to see this feather.

Fra Cipolla, having made a hearty breakfast and had a little nap, got up shortly after none, and marking the great concourse of country-folk that were come to see the feather, sent word to Guccio Imbratta to go up there with the bells, and bring with him the wallet. Guccio, though 'twas with difficulty that he tore himself away from the kitchen and Nuta, hied him up with the things required; and though, when he got up, he was winded, for he was corpulent with drinking nought but water, he did Fra Cipolla's bidding by going to the church door and ringing the bells amain. When all the people were gathered about the door, Fra Cipolla, all unwitting that aught of his was missing, began his sermon, and after much said in glorification of himself, caused the confiteor to be recited with great solemnity, and two torches to be lit by way of preliminary to the showing of the feather of the Angel Gabriel: he then bared his head, carefully unfolded the taffeta, and took out the casket, which, after a few prefatory words in praise and laudation of the Angel Gabriel and his relic, he opened. When he saw that it contained nought but coals, he did not suspect Guccio Balena of playing the trick, for he knew that he was not clever enough, nor did he curse him, that his carelessness had allowed another to play it, but he only imprecated himself, that he had committed his things to the keeping of one whom he knew to be "negligent and disobedient, reckless and witless." Nevertheless, he changed not colour, but with face and hands upturned to heaven, he said in a voice that all might hear:—"O God, blessed be Thy might for ever and ever." Then, closing the casket and turning to the people:—"Ladies and gentlemen," he said, "you are to know that when I was yet a very young man, I was sent by my superior into those parts where the sun rises, and I was expressly bidden to search until I should find the Privileges of Porcellana, which, though they cost nothing to seal, are of much more use to others than to us. On which errand I set forth, taking my departure from Venice, and traversing the Borgo de' Greci, and thence on horseback the realm of Algarve, and so by Baldacca I came to Parione, whence, somewhat athirst, I after a while got to Sardinia. But wherefore go I about to enumerate all the lands in which I pursued my quest? Having passed the straits of San Giorgio, I arrived at Truffia and Buffia, countries thickly populated and with great nations, whence I pursued my journey to Menzongna, where I met with many of our own brethren, and of other religious not a few, intent one and all on eschewing hardship for the love of God, making little account of others' toil, so they might pursue their own advantage, and paying in nought but unminted coin throughout the length and breadth of the country; and so I came to the land of Abruzzi, where the men and women go in pattens on the mountains, and clothe the hogs with their own entrails; and a little further on I found folk that carried bread in staves and wine in sacks. And leaving them, I arrived at the mountains of the Bachi, where all the waters run downwards. In short I penetrated so far that I came at last to India Pastinaca, where I swear to you by the habit that I wear, that I saw pruning-hooks fly: a thing that none would believe that had not seen it. Whereof be my witness that I lie not Maso del Saggio, that great merchant, whom I found there cracking nuts, and selling the shells by retail! However, not being able to find that whereof I was in quest, because from thence one must travel by water, I turned back, and so came at length to the Holy Land, where in summer cold bread costs four deniers, and hot bread is to be had for nothing. And there I found the venerable father Nonmiblasmetesevoipiace, the most worshipful Patriarch of Jerusalem; who out of respect for the habit that I have ever worn, to wit, that of Baron Master St. Antony, was pleased to let me see all the holy relics that he had by him, which were so many that, were I to enumerate them all, I should not come to the end of them in some miles. However, not to disappoint you, I will tell you a few of them. In the first place, then, he showed me the finger of the Holy Spirit, as whole and entire as it ever was, and the tuft of the Seraph that appeared to St Francis, and one of the nails

of the Cherubim, and one of the ribs of the Verbum Caro
hie thee to the casement, and some of the vestments of the
Holy Catholic Faith, and some of the rays of the star that
appeared to the Magi in the East, and a phial of the sweat
of St Michael a-battling with the Devil, and the jaws of
death of St Lazarus, and other relics. And for that I gave
him a liberal supply of the acclivities of Monte Morello
in the vulgar and some chapters of Caprezio, of which he
had long been in quest, he was pleased to let me participate
in his holy relics, and gave me one of the teeth of the Holy
Cross, and in a small phial a bit of the sound of the bells of
Solomon's temple, and this feather of the Angel Gabriel,
whereof I have told you, and one of the pattens of San
Gherardo da Villa Magna, which, not long ago, I gave at
Florence to Gherardo di Bonsi, who holds him in prodigious
veneration. He also gave me some of the coals with which
the most blessed martyr, St Lawrence, was roasted. All
which things I devoutly brought thence, and have them all
safe. True it is that my superior has not hitherto permitted
me to show them, until he should be certified that they are
genuine. However, now that this is avouched by certain
miracles wrought by them, of which we have tidings by
letter from the Patriarch, he has given me leave to show
them. But, fearing to trust them to another, I always carry
them with me; and to tell you the truth, I carry the feather
of the Angel Gabriel, lest it should get spoiled, in a casket,
and the coals, with which St Lawrence was roasted, in
another casket; which caskets are so like the one to the
other, that not seldom I mistake one for the other, which
has befallen me on this occasion; for, whereas I thought to
have brought with me the casket wherein is the feather, I
have brought instead that which contains the coals. Nor
deem I this mischance; nay, methinks, 'tis by interposition
of God, and that He Himself put the casket of coals in my
hand, for I mind me that the feast of St Lawrence falls but
two days hence. Wherefore God, being minded that by
showing you the coals, with which he was roasted, I should
rekindle in your souls the devotion that you ought to feel

towards him, guided my hand, not to the feather which I meant to take, but to the blessed coals that were extinguished by the humours that exuded from that most holy body. And so, blessed children bare your heads and devoutly draw nigh to see them. But first of all I would have you know, that whoso has the sign of the cross made upon him with these coals, may live secure for the whole of the ensuing year, that fire shall not touch him, that he feel it now."

Having so said, the friar, chanting a hymn in praise of St Lawrence, opened the casket, and showed the coals. Whereon the foolish crowd gazed a while in awe and reverent wonder, and then came pressing forward in a mighty throng about Fra Cipolla with offerings beyond their wont, each and all praying him to touch them with the coals. Wherefore Fra Cipolla took the coals in his hand, and set about making on their white blouses, and on their doublets, and on the veils of the women crosses as big as might be, averring the while that whatever the coals might thus lose would be made good to them again in the casket, as he had often proved. On this wise, to his exceeding great profit, he marked all the folk of Certaldo with the cross, and, thanks to his ready wit and resource, had his laugh at those, who by robbing him of the feather, thought to make a laughing-stock of him. They, indeed, being among his hearers, and marking his novel expedient, and how voluble he was, and what a long story he made of it, laughed till they thought their jaws would break; and, when the congregation was dispersed, they went up to him, and never so merrily told him what they had done, and returned him his feather; which next year proved no less lucrative to him than that day the coals had been.

BOCCACCIO *The Decameron*


When Fabrizio del Dongo, whom we met a little earlier on, became Archbishop of Parma, he did not, for all that, lose his love-passion for Clelia Conti—the Marchesa. To make contact with her, he began preaching in various churches in the city. His sermons drew larger and larger crowds. At last they met and the Archbishop was in an ecstasy of love.

## Fabrizio's Sermon and Meeting with Clelia

Fabrizio appeared in the pulpit; he was so thin, so pale, so *consumed*, that Clelia's eyes immediately filled with tears. Fabrizio uttered a few words, then stopped, as though his voice had suddenly failed; he tried in vain to begin various sentences; he turned round and took up a sheet of paper:

"Brethren," he said, "an unhappy soul and one well worthy of all your pity requests you, through my lips, to pray for the ending of his torments, which will cease only with his life."

Fabrizio read the rest of his paper very slowly; but the expression of his voice was such that before he was half-way through the prayer, everyone was weeping, even Gonzo. "At any rate, I shall not be noticed," thought the Marchesa, bursting into tears.

While he was reading from the paper, Fabrizio found two or three ideas concerning the state of the unhappy man for whom he had come to beg the prayers of the faithful. Presently thoughts came to him in abundance. While he appeared to be addressing the public, he spoke only to the Marchesa. He ended his discourse a little sooner than was usual, because, in spite of his efforts to control them, his tears got the better of him to such a point that he was no longer able to pronounce his words in an intelligible manner. The good judges found this sermon strange but quite equal, in pathos at least, to the famous sermon preached with the lighted candles. As for Clelia, no sooner had she heard the first ten lines of the prayer read by Fabrizio than it seemed to her an atrocious crime to have been able to spend fourteen months without seeing him. On her return home she took to her bed, to be able to think of Fabrizio with perfect freedom; and next morning, at an early hour, Fabrizio received a note couched in the following terms:

"We rely upon your honour; find four *bravi,* of whose discretion you can be sure, and tomorrow, when midnight sounds from the Steccata, be by a little door which bears the number 19, in the Strada San Paolo. Remember that you may be attacked, do not come alone."

On recognising that heavenly script, Fabrizio fell on his knees and burst into tears. "At last," he cried, "after fourteen months and eight days! Farewell to preaching."

It would take too long to describe all the varieties of folly to which the hearts of Fabrizio and Clelia were a prey that day. The little door indicated in the note was none other than that of the orangery of the *palazzo* Crescenzi, and ten times in the day Fabrizio found an excuse to visit it. He armed himself, and alone, shortly before midnight, with a rapid step, was passing by the door when, to his inexpressible joy, he heard a well-known voice say in a very low whisper:

"Come in here, friend of my heart."

Fabrizio entered cautiously and found himself actually in the orangery, but opposite a window heavily barred which stood three or four feet above the ground. The darkness was intense. Fabrizio had heard a slight sound in this window, and was exploring the bars with his hand, when he felt another hand, slipped through the bars, take hold of his and carry it to a pair of lips which gave it a kiss.

"It is I," said a dear voice, "who have come here to tell you that I love you, and to ask you if you are willing to obey me."

One may imagine the answer, the joy, the astonishment, of Fabrizio; after the first transports, Clelia said to him:

"I have made a vow to the Madonna, as you know, never to see you; that is why I receive you in this profound darkness. I wish you to understand clearly that, should you ever force me to look at you in the daylight, all would be over between us. But first of all, I do not wish you to preach before Annetta Marini, and do not go and think that it was I who was so foolish as to have an armchair carried into the House of God."

"My dear angel, I shall never preach before anyone; I have been preaching only in the hope that one day I might see you."

"Do not speak like that, remember that it is not permitted to me to see you."

STENDHAL The Charterhouse of Parma

# Italians in Love

M Y LAST quotation might seem as fitted to be put under the heading of love as of religion. But my headings are rough and ready. All parts of Italian life interpenetrate, just as all Italians, from Naples and Venice, Turin and Rome, are constantly travelling and settling in new cities. And so how could those two most vital urges, religion and passion-love, fail to interlink? Under the humane sky of Italy their connection is at times disconcerting. The other day, in a church in Rome, I found myself standing next to a young man of the scooter kind, in his rather overdressed Sunday best. He appeared to be praying passionately and his fingers were turning over and over without ceasing. I thought he was saying the rosary, but when I looked down at his hands I saw that what he was fingering was a little red horn (nowadays they are made of plastic), the talisman against the evil eye and all diseases. He might have been praying for his mother's recovery from an operation; but equally he might have been asking the universal Mother, the Madonna, to give him the girl he loved, or to send his rival, Dario, back to Sicily, or to prevent them having a baby too soon, or to make them both as fruitful as uncursed fig trees and populate the face of the earth like Abraham (he would not have heard of Abraham, but the principle is the same).

In this selection, too, I have drawn a lot on Stendhal. But I would like to say once more that his genius lay in seeing things from the outside. He liked stressing the operatic, baroque and passionate aspects of Italian life, because he was always gunning against those cold and calculating fish, his fellow-countrymen.

## *Lovers and Mistresses Living in the Present*

Save only in money-matters, the blandest unconcern with the future is an outstanding characteristic of Italy;

every waking thought is taken up with the present instant. A woman will remain faithful to her lover fully eighteen months or two years, while he is travelling abroad; but he *must* write to her. Should he meet his death, she is plunged into despair, not for any thought of future anguish, but overwhelmed by instantaneous sorrow. This immediacy of sensation explains the rarity of lovers' suicides. There is a saying among lovers, that if a man is called upon to live several months parted from his mistress, he should bid her farewell on the verge of a quarrel.

STENDHAL Rome, Naples and Florence

Here is another typically Stendhalian passage about passion. We are very far from what Léon Bloy denounced as bourgeois love in Paris, in which the sacrosanct franc plays a crucial role, even if only as background.

## A Baroque Love Affair

*Near MELITO, 28th May.* Some few months since, a married woman of this country, renowned for her un-wavering piety no less than for her uncommon beauty, did so far falter in the path of virtue as to grant an assignation to her lover in a forest remote among the mountain, some six miles distant from her village. The lover was fortunate in the enjoyment of his mistress' favours. Yet, no sooner had this instant of madness passed away, than the full hideousness of her sin bore down upon her guilty soul: motionless she remained, plunged in oppressive silence. "Why so cold, so distant?" enquired the lover. "I was dreaming," replied his mistress, "of the means we might employ to meet again tomorrow; this woodman's hut, long since abandoned, here where the forest is dark, is the most fitting spot." The lover took his leave; but the unhappy woman made no move to return to her village; instead, she passed the night in the heart of the forest, and whiled away the hours (as later she confessed) partly in prayer, partly in digging two graves set one against the other. The dawn broke; and ere long, with the daylight, came her lover, only to meet his death at the hands of his mistress, who, as he believed, did worship the very earth on which he trod. Still prey to the same remorse, the poor, tortured creature proceeded to bury her lover with the greatest care and reverence; then, retracing her footsteps to the village, she made her confession to the priest and embraced her children. Lastly, she returned once more into the forest, where she was later discovered, stretched lifeless in the hollow of the trench which she had dug beside the grave which held her lover.

STENDHAL *Rome, Naples and Florence*

Here we have Machiavelli, as a lover and on love.

## *Machiavelli on Love*

My dear friend, these further reports about your Roman love affair kept me in good spirits and lifted a thousand burdens from my mind as I read and shared your joys and torments—for the one can hardly exist without the other. And now, Fortune has actually given me the opportunity of answering you in kind, for here in the country I have met a creature so charming, so delicate, so noble both in character and behaviour that however much I praise and love her, her deserts are higher. I must, as you did me, tell you how this love began, about the nets it caught me with, where it stretched them, and what stuff they were made of. Understand then that they were nets of gold, laid among flowers, woven by Venus, so soft and gentle that though an insensitive heart could have broken them I had no wish to, and I enjoyed myself so long there that the soft threads hardened, fastening into knots that can never be undone. And do not imagine that Love tried to snare me in the old familiar ways; he knew that these would not be enough and used extraordinary means, which I did not know how

to guard against—nor did I wish to. Suffice it, then, that
although rising fifty years of age this does not perturb me,
nor do rough ways tire me, nor the darkness of the nights
make me afraid. All is plain: I adapt myself to every
inclination however different and against my nature. And
though I can see that I am letting myself in for trouble, all
the same I find such sweetness in it both from the contemplation of that rare and delicate face and from having
put aside any memory of my worries, that even if I could
free myself I would not, for anything in the world. I have
given up, then, thoughts of matters grand and grave; I take
no more pleasure in reading about the ancient world nor
arguing about the modern; all this has given place to the
conversation of love, for which thanks be to Venus and
the whole Cyprian isle. So if you want to write anything
about your lady, do so, and discuss other things with those
who value them more and understand them better, for they
have brought me nothing but loss, while in love I have
always found pleasure and profit. *Valete*.

NICCOLÒ MACHIAVELLI
Letter to Francesco Vettori, August, 1514

*De amore vestro,* let me remind you that Love only torments those who try to bind him when he flies into their
laps, or try to clip his wings; being a young and fickle lad
he digs out eyes, liver and heart together. But those who
rejoice when he comes to them, and play with him, let him
go as he pleases and welcome him when he returns, they
will always be treated well and favoured by him and
triumph by submitting to his rule. And so, my friend, do
not try to fetter a creature that flies, nor clip the wings of a
being who can grow a thousand feathers for every one he
loses; and in this way you will be happy.

NICCOLÒ MACHIAVELLI
Letter to Francesco Vettori, June, 1514

Once again, as in the story of Abelard and Héloïse, passionate
love lives on the edge of religion and the convent.

## The Romantic and Precocious Duchessa

In the company of my sixteen-year-old *duchessa,* I visited the collection of paintings owned by *il cavaliere* Ghigi. My fair companion, I learned, was involved in a situation romantic enough in all conscience to form the plot of a novel, yet too delicate, perhaps, to be used as such within the framework of our present conventions. Prince Corvi, being in love with *la contessina* Carolina, the mother of my young *duchessa,* yet tasting all the bitterness of jealousy, for that he could find no means to loosen the tender bonds of her affection for the *cavaliere* P . . . , decided to reveal the secret of this *liaison* to the lady's husband, an amiable-tempered fellow, who refused to believe a word of this ill-timed denunciation. Baffled at the first attempt, the Prince resolved to go a step further, and repeated his denunciation to the *contessina's* daughters, two charming and innocent creatures of fifteen or sixteen summers, who were most tenderly attached to their mother. These two unhappy children were so distressed by the discovery, that they privately resolved together to take the veil; they grew embarrassed in their mother's presence, and durst no longer speak a word to her. At long last, the elder of the two, falling upon her knees at her mother's feet, burst into tears and unburdened herself of all the tale of Prince Corvi's denunciation, together with the secret of their common resolution to enter a convent, lest they should suffer the contamination of a *woman taken in adultery.* Imagine the atrocious dilemma of the *contessina*—a mother torn between her adoration for her lover and her implacable sense of honour. By good fortune, she retained sufficient presence of mind to deny the whole story. This little narrative—which takes some twenty minutes in the telling —is perhaps the most beautiful and most moving episodes I have encountered in a year.

STENDHAL Rome, Naples and Florence

It is not easy to equate two sides of the Italian character when confronted with passion-love. There is the immediate pursuit of passion's dictates whatever the cost—and the cost can be very high. The Italian man caught up in the appalling web of obsessive passion longs to get free from the tyranny of it and become himself again. But every action of the day and night is governed by thoughts of the beloved. In France or Britain such passion might be called "weakness". The gods must judge: at least we are no longer slaves to "national" prejudices, we realise "nations" are man-made and unlikely to last much longer. But side by side with the passion can go a great deal of "Machiavellian" calculation, which offends romantics. Italy is not a romantic country.

## *Mosca and the Sanseverina's Marriage*

At the degree of intimacy which in Italy follows love, there was no longer any obstacle in the nature of vanity between the lovers. It was therefore with the most perfect simplicity that Mosca said to the woman he adored:

"I have two or three plans of conduct to offer you, all pretty well thought out; I have been thinking of nothing else for the last three months.

"First: I hand in my resignation, and we retire to a quiet life at Milan or Florence or Naples or wherever you please. We have an income of 15,000 francs, apart from the Prince's generosity, which will continue for some time, more or less.

"Secondly: You condescend to come to the place in which I have some authority; you buy a property, Sacca, for example, a charming house in the middle of a forest, commanding the valley of the Po; you can have the contract signed within a week from now. The Prince then attaches you to his court. But here I can see an immense objection. You will be well received at court; no-one would think of refusing, with me there; besides, the Princess imagines she is unhappy, and I have recently rendered her certain services with an eye to your future. But I must remind you of one paramount objection: the Prince is a bigoted churchman, and, as you already know, ill luck will have it that I am a married man. From which will arise a million minor unpleasantnesses. You are a widow; it is a

*St Peter's*

In the heart of turbulent, twentieth-century
Rome, the rest and silence of the old *Via Sacra*

*Rome is a city of fountains—baths of the gods*

*The ancient Capitol was re-designed by Michelangelo*

fine title which would have to be exchanged for another, and this brings me to my third proposal.

"One might find a new husband who would not be a nuisance. But first of all he would have to be considerably advanced in years, for why should you deny me the hope of some day succeeding him? Very well, I have made this curious arrangement with the Duca Sanseverina-Taxis, who, of course, does not know the name of his future Duchessa. He knows only that she will make him an Ambassador and will procure him the Grand Cordon which his father had and the lack of which makes him the most unhappy of mortals. Apart from this, the Duca is by no means an absolute idiot; he gets his clothes and wigs from Paris. He is not in the least the sort of man who would do anything *deliberately* mean, he seriously believes that honour consists in his having a Cordon, and he is ashamed of his riches. He came to me a year ago proposing to found a hospital, in order to get this Cordon; I laughed at him then, but he did not by any means laugh at me when I made him a proposal of marriage; my first condition was, you can understand, that he must never set foot again in Parma."

"But do you know that what you are proposing is highly immoral?" said the Contessa.

"No more immoral than everything else that is done at our court and a score of others. Absolute Power has this advantage, that it sanctifies everything in the eyes of the public: what harm can there be in a thing that nobody notices? Our policy for the next twenty years is going to consist in fear of the Jacobins—and such fear, too! Every year, we shall fancy ourselves on the eve of '93. You will hear, I hope, the fine speeches I make on the subject at my receptions! They are beautiful! Everything that can in any way reduce this fear will be *supremely moral* in the eyes of the nobles and the bigots. And you see, at Parma, everyone who is not either a noble or a bigot is in prison, or is packing up to go there; you may be quite sure that this marriage will not be thought odd among us until the day on which I am disgraced. This arrangement involves no dishonesty towards anyone; that is the essential thing, it seems to me. The Prince, on whose favour we are trading, has placed only one condition on his consent, which is that the future Duchessa shall be of noble birth. Last year my office, all told, brought me in 107,000 francs; my total income would therefore be 122,000; I invested 20,000 at Lyons. Very well, choose for yourself; either, a life of luxury based on our having 122,000 francs to spend, which, at Parma, go as far as at least 400,000 at Milan; but with this marriage which will give you the name of a passable man on whom you will never set eyes after you leave the altar; or else the simple middle-class existence on 15,000 francs at Florence or Naples, for I am of your opinion, you have been too much admired at Milan; we should be persecuted here by envy, which might perhaps succeed in souring our tempers. Our grand life at Parma will, I hope, have some touches of novelty, even in your eyes which have seen the court of Prince Eugène: you would be wise to try it before shutting the door on it for ever. Do not think that I am seeking to influence your opinion. As for me, my mind is quite made up: I would rather live on a fourth floor with you than continue that grand life by myself."

STENDHAL *The Charterhouse of Parma*

Italians also disconcert people from more northern countries by their apparent absence of "sense of sin" or "guilt". Things are much more complicated than that really, of course. Readers whose background tends to be Puritan should remember that it is hard for Italians to think of pleasure as wrong. But there is a golden mean, and Benvenuto's adventure with the prostitute was hardly pleasant.

### Women and the Plague

Still the plague raged on for many months, but I had kept it at a distance. Many of my comrades had died, yet I remained safe and free from infection. Now it happened

one night that one of my intimate acquaintances brought a
Bolognese prostitute called Faustina home to supper. She
was a very beautiful woman, though she was about thirty
years old; and she had with her a little maid of thirteen or
fourteen. Now as Faustina was my friend's property, I
would not have had any dealings with her for all the gold
in the world; and although she said she was much in love
with me, I never swerved from my loyalty to my friend.
But after they were in bed, I ran off with the little maid, who
was as fresh as fresh; and it would have been a bad job for
her if her mistress had known. So I spent a much pleasanter
night than if I had had the mistress Faustina. Next day
when dinner time came near, I was tired and hungry as
after a walk of many miles. Then I was seized with a violent
headache; swellings rose in my left arm, and I discovered a
carbuncle just by my left wrist-bone. Every one in the
house was terrified; my friend, the big cow, and the little
calf all fled away, and I was left alone with my poor little
shop-boy, who refused to leave me. I felt suffocated, and
I looked on myself as a dead man. Just then the father of
my apprentice passed by, who was Cardinal Jacobacci's
household physician. The boy ran out to meet him, crying,
"Come, father, and see Benvenuto, who is in bed, and not
very well." Not thinking what my illness might be, he
came in at once, felt my pulse, and then too clearly saw
what he would fain have been blind to. Turning quickly to
his son, he cried, "O you faithless boy, you have ruined
me! How can I ever again go into the Cardinal's presence?"
To which the boy replied, "My master, father, is worth
more than all the cardinals in Rome." Then turning to me,
the doctor said, "Now that I am here I will treat you. Only
of one thing I warn you, that if you have been with a
woman, there is no help for you." To this I answered, "I
was with one last night." "With what sort of creature?"
asked the doctor, "and how long?" "The whole night," I
replied, "and with a very young girl." Then seeing he had
spoken rashly, he made haste to add, "Since the sores are
still fresh and not putrid, and since there has been no

delay about the remedy, do not be over-anxious, for I certainly hope to cure you." When he had treated me and gone away, there came in one of my dearest friends, called Giovanni Rigogli, who grieved over my illness, and at my solitary condition. "Depend upon it, Benvenuto, my friend," he said, "I shall never leave you till I see you cured." Then I told him not to come near me, for I was doomed. Only I begged him to be good enough to take a quantity of crown pieces that were in a little box near my bed, and, as soon as God should have taken me from the world, to send them to my poor father. He was to write to him cheerfully how I, too, had succumbed to the common fate of that terrible season. But my dear friend swore he would not be parted from me for anything; and whatever should come to pass, were it good or ill, he knew quite well what it behoved him to do for his friend. So we went on by the help of God; and, thanks to the marvellous remedies which were applied, a great improvement set in, and I came happily out of that terrible illness.

BENVENUTO CELLINI Memoirs

In this next quotation Mr Aubrey Menen is writing particularly about Neapolitans in love. In Naples words and gestures are more immediately expressive, more *theatrical,* than in other parts of Italy. But for all that, this situation is a peninsular one, and women from northern countries who go to Italy looking for cinema romance should be warned about what they are in for.

Another thing we must never forget is that the family is still a living institution in Italy, with rich and poor alike—the family interest will always win in the end. This includes spontaneous love for ageing parents, for brothers and sisters, for children and even for uncles, aunts and cousins. I know nothing about psycho-analysis, but if there is hardly any work for psycho-analysts in Italy I am sure there are more reasons for this than the fact that children are not inhibited by their parents for the sake of some abstract ideal—or for a parental need for self torture. In London I have known numbers of people say, "I hated my father", or, "I hated my mother". I have never known an Italian who said this.

As for the girls, it is different. Everything depends on whether they are plain or beautiful. If they are plain, they will lead dull or worthy lives, producing rather more children than they should and growing old too fast. But if they are beautiful (and very many are) they can confidently look forward to the experience of the *avventura*. The bold glance, the provocative carriage of a good-looking Neapolitan girl stems from this expectation, and although the *avventura* nearly always ends in disappointment for her, it is very flattering while it lasts.

The *avventura* is a Neapolitan love affair, which follows a fixed pattern. Every young man in Naples who claims to be a man at all is expected to have at least one but preferably several *avventura* before he gets married. This "adventure" consists in falling passionately in love with a girl and flinging himself in wild abandon at her feet. Having selected the woman, he goes through a ritual of abject adoration which has won for the Neapolitan the reputation, outside Naples, of being the most passionate lover in the world. The Neapolitans, themselves, do not think they are. Let me describe what really happens.

The beginning of the adoration is the *passeggiata* or walk, almost invariably, except among the very poor, done in a car or a rowboat. During the walk, the man hangs adoringly over the object of his passion, sighing from time to time at her beauty. If she drops a flower, it is seized as a keepsake. Endless snapshots are taken in which both parties pose in romantic attitudes. Passers-by will be freely called upon to take pictures of the lovers together.

All this is done in beauty spots, such as the craggy coast of the Sorrento peninsula, among the pines of Ischia, or in picturesque fishing villages. Foreign girls are often surprised to find that these places are often full of people, whereas in other countries lovers seek out solitude. They do not, however, in Naples, and this is because of the *bella figura*, or the need to cut a fine figure.

The Neapolitan lover, having captured his girl, wants

everybody to see him at work adoring her. Therefore, like the Queen of England, he dresses in light colours, so that he can easily be picked out. He will describe an outing by saying, "I took her to Positano. We had a wonderful time. I looked well in my new white shoes." Indeed, in a decade of living in the Naples area and (it would seem) hearing men incessantly talking about women, I cannot remember one occasion on which the man described what the woman was wearing. The Neapolitan on an *avventura* is a peacock.

If the woman, for understandable reasons, insists on an isolated spot, the man will go, because a woman must be obeyed, but if there is nobody about, he may very well sulk. It is the *bella figura,* too, which accounts for a habit which romantic women visitors to this area have often commented upon. Her escort will lead up, with elaborate and subtle tactics, to a tender moment. Then, when he is poised over her lips, like as not he will glance at his wrist-watch and say, "Excuse me, I must make a telephone call." This is not wholly a lie, but it is not an evasion. He will actually telephone somebody, usually a male friend, and then boast elaborately about what he is doing with the girl, including hints as to what he plans to do further in the next hour. He likes to make his call from as public a spot as possible. Telephones in bars in Italy are not enclosed. Everyone can hear a conversation. If by chance they cannot, he will raise his voice till they can. He thus makes a doubly beautiful figure.

On each of these outings, he will send off numbers of picture postcards to his friends, partly to show off, partly as evidence that the lovers have really been where they say they have. Snapshots will be later posted off in batches, or handed round for the same purpose.

Then comes the exchange of rings, invariably very cheap ones. The man, to express his godlike devotion, will place a second ring on top of the first. This is known as the "faithful" ring, and it is the climax of the pursuit. During it all, apart from time out for glances at the watch and scribbling postcards, the woman has been overwhelmed with praise, admiration, declarations of passion and (perhaps, though not necessarily) love-making. The man now relaxes, and waits for the woman to fling herself upon him and say she cannot live without him. If she does anything of the sort, Heaven help her. The *avventura* is over and her lover will begin to treat her as the woman she really is. She is no longer a goddess: she will be observed with a remarkably cold and realistic eye. The game being over, the next step can only be marriage, and for the Neapolitan there may be profit and comfort in matrimony, but there is no romance.

If she resists the temptation to give in to her lover, she will get the same chilling douche. Her ardent admirer of the previous weeks or days becomes an irritable, quarrelsome man, perpetually anxious to be off and away. She does not understand that he is about to enjoy the last exquisite pleasures of the game—the part that is played, so to speak, in the locker room with the men. He is about to suffer, under the eyes of his envious companions, the pangs of a broken heart. He is distracted, he listens with tears in his eyes when orchestras play, he forswears coffee in case it should excite him to do something desperate. His companions, his family and his neighbours watch him with appreciation. They are perfectly well aware that he has probably lost the woman's address, forgotten what she looks like and is calling her, mentally, by the name of some other woman.

AUBREY MENEN
*Speaking the Language Like a Native*

# Rome

ROME ONLY became the capital of Italy in 1870—before that it had been the kingdom of the Popes for a thousand years. This explains its contrasts. What is most traditional and living in its architecture is papal. Under the Popes, Rome became a poem in stone, set in the deserted grasslands of the campagna or surrounding country. It was then a small city, with only about two hundred thousand inhabitants—far smaller than Naples or Milan—whereas today it has more than ten times as many inhabitants. There are very few real Romans left. The old papal city is now called "the Centre"—*il Centro*—a jewel set in a mass of glass and concrete blocks of flats, garages, offices that might be in Los Angeles or Buenos Aires. The characterless city is spreading tentacularly over the campagna, towards the sea and Ostia, towards the Alban hills. The great change has come in the last ten or fifteen years.

## *Arrival in Rome*

When we turned the summit above Viterbo and opened on the view on the other side, it might be called the first approach to Rome. At the distance of more than forty miles, it was, of course, impossible to see the town, and besides, the distance was hazy; but we were looking on the scene of Roman history; we were standing on the outward edge of the frame of the great picture; and though the features of it were not to be traced distinctly, yet we had the consciousness that they were before us. Here, too, we first saw the Mediterranean, the Alban hills, I think, in the remote distance, and just beneath us on the left, Soracte, an outlier of the Apennines, which has got to the right

bank of the Tiber, and stands out by itself most magnifi-
cently. Close under us, in front, was the Ciminian lake, the
crater of an extinct volcano, and lying like a beautiful
mirror stretched out before us. Then there was the grand
beauty of Italian scenery, the depth of the valleys, the endless variety of the mountain outline, and the towns perched
upon the mountain summits, and this now seen under a
mottled sky, which threw an ever varying light and shadow
over the valley beneath, and all the freshness of the young
spring. We descended along one of the rims of this lake
to Ronciglione, and, from thence, still descending on the
whole, to Monterosi. Here the famous Campagna begins,
and it certainly is one of the most striking tracts of country
I ever beheld. It is by no means a perfect flat, except
between Rome and the sea; but rather like the Bagshot
Heath country, ridges of hills, with intermediate valleys,
and the road often running between high steep banks, and
sometimes crossing sluggish streams sunk in a deep bed.
All these banks are overgrown with broom, now in full
flower; and the same plant was luxuriant everywhere.
There seemed no apparent reason why the country should
be so desolate; the grass was growing richly everywhere.
There was no marsh anywhere visible, but all looked as
fresh and healthy as any of our chalk downs in England.
But it is a wide wilderness; no villages, scarcely any houses,
and here and there a lonely ruin of a single square tower,
which I suppose used to serve as strongholds for men and
cattle in the plundering warfare of the middle ages. It was
after crowning the top of one of these lines of hills, a little
on the Roman side of Baccono, at five minutes after six,
according to my watch, that we had the first view of Rome
itself. I expected to see St Peter's rising above the line of
the horizon, as York Minster does; but instead of that it
was within the horizon, and so was much less conspicuous,
and from the nature of the ground it looked mean and
stumpy. Nothing else marked the site of the city, but the
trees of the gardens and a number of white villas specking
the opposite bank of the Tiber for some little distance above
the town and then suddenly ceasing. But the whole scene

that burst upon our view, when taken in all its parts, was most interesting. Full in front rose the Alban hills, the white villas on their sides distinctly visible, even at that distance, which was more than thirty miles. On the left were the Apennines and Tivoli was distinctly to be seen on the summit of its mountain, on one of the lowest and nearest parts of the chain. On the right, and all before us, lay the Campagna, whose perfectly level outline was succeeded by that of the sea, which was scarcely more so. It began now to get dark, and as there is hardly any twilight, it was dark soon after we left La Storta, the last post before you enter Rome. The air blew fresh and cool, and we had a pleasant drive over the remaining part of the Campagna, till we descended into the valley of the Tiber, and crossed it by the Milvian bridge. About two miles further on we reached the walls of Rome, and entered it by the Porta del Popolo.

MATTHEW ARNOLD

But lovers of Rome began lamenting the changes before the end of the nineteenth century.

## *Desecration in Rome*

Twenty-two years of Sardinian rule (1870–92) have done more for the destruction of Rome than all the invasions of the Goths and Vandals. If the government, the municipality, and, it must be confessed, the Roman aristocracy, had been united together since 1870, with the *sole* object of anni-hilating the beauty and interest of Rome, they could not have done it more effectually. The old charm is gone for ever, the whole aspect of the city is changed, and the pictur-esqueness of former days must now be sought in such obscure corners as have escaped the hands of the spoiler. The glorious gardens of the villa Negroni, villa Corsini and villa Ludovisi have been annihilated; many precious street memorials of medieval history have been swept away; the sacred Promenade of the Sun has been desecrated; ancient convents have been levelled with the ground or turned into barracks; historic churches have been yellow-washed or modernised; every tree of importance in the city—including the noble ilexes of Christina of Sweden—have been cut down; the cloisters of Michelangelo have been walled up; the pagan ruins have been denuded of all that gave them picturesqueness or beauty; and several of the finest fountains have been pulled down or bereaved of half their water. The Palace of the Caesars is stripped of all the flowers and shrubs which formerly adorned it. The glorious view from the Pincio has been destroyed by the hideous barracks built between the Tiber and St Peter's. The Tiber itself has been diverted from its exquisitely picturesque course, to the destruction, amongst many other interesting memorials, of the lovely Farnesina gardens and the fatal injury of the inestimable frescoes in the palace. The hideous new bridges block out the best views on the river banks. The baths of Caracalla, which, till 1870, were one of the most beautiful spots in the world, are now scarcely more attractive than the ruins of a London warehouse. Many of the most interesting temples have been dwarfed by the vulgarest and tallest of modern buildings. Even the Colosseum has been rendered a centre for fever by aimless excavations, and has been deprived not only of its shrines, but of its marvellous flora, though in dragging out the roots of its shrubs more of the building was destroyed than would have fallen naturally in five centuries.

AUGUSTUS HARE *Walks in Rome*

Henry James was another foreigner who noticed the changes.

## *The New Rome*

A traveller acquainted with the fully papal Rome, coming back any time during the past winter [1873] must have immediately noticed that something momentous had happened—something hostile to the elements of picture and colour and "style". My first warning was that ten minutes after my arrival I found myself face to face with a newspaper stand. The impossibility in the other days of having anything in the journalistic line but the *Osservatore Romano* and the *Voce della Verità* used to seem to me much connected with the extraordinary leisure of thought and stillness of mind to which the place admitted you. But now the slender piping of the Voice of Truth is stifled by the raucous note of eventide vendors of the *Capitale,* the *Libertà* and the *Fanfulla*; and Rome reading unexpurgated news is another Rome indeed. For every subscriber to the *Libertà* there may well be an antique masker and reveller less. As striking a sign of the new régime is the extraordinary increase of population. The Corso was always a well-filled street, but now it's a perpetual crush. I never cease to wonder where the newcomers are lodged, and how such spotless flowers of fashion as the gentlemen who stare at the carriages can bloom in the atmosphere of those *camere mobigliate* of which I have had glimpses. This, however, is their own question, and bravely enough they meet it. They proclaimed somehow, to the first freshness of my wonder, as I say, that by force of numbers Rome has been secularised. An Italian dandy is a figure visually to reckon with, but these goodly throngs of them scarce offered compensation for the absent monsignori, treading the streets in their purple stockings and followed by the solemn servants who returned on their behalf the bows of the meaner sort; for the mourning gear of the cardinals' coaches that formerly glittered with scarlet and swung with the weight of the footmen clinging behind; for the certainty that you'll not, by the best of traveller's luck, meet the Pope sitting deep in the shadow of his great chariot with uplifted fingers like some inaccessible idol in his shrine. You may meet the King indeed, who is as ugly, as imposingly ugly, as some idols, though not so inaccessible. The other day as I passed the Quirinal he drove up in a low carriage with a single attendant; and a group of men and women who had been waiting near the gate rushed at him with a number of folded papers. The carriage slackened pace and he pocketed their offerings with a business-like air—that of a good-natured man accepting handbills at a street-corner. Here was a monarch at his palace gate receiving petitions from his subjects—being adjured to right their wrongs. The scene ought to have thrilled me, but somehow it had no more intensity than a woodcut in an illustrated newspaper. Homely I should call it at most; admirably so, certainly, for there were lately few sovereigns standing, I believe, with whom their people enjoyed these filial hand-to-hand relations. The King this year, however, has had as little to do with the Carnival as the Pope, and the innkeepers and Americans have marked it for their own.

HENRY JAMES Italian Hours

Here is yet another complaint.

## The Idolatrous Monument

January, 1913.

My dearest Bastian. You, who have seen the oriental sun, can hardly perhaps imagine the joy I take in the mere Italian—the reflected light from one side of the street to the other, the darkness of the cypress and the ilex in the sun. I could not rest for the beauty of it yesterday, and I wandered everywhere, except to St Peter's, which is for today. This is my *sixth* visit to Rome, yet it is always a surprise.

The temple to the divine Victor Emmanuel, as I call this idolatrous monument, is even worse, now it is finished, than I expected. It is beautiful in itself, but it is out of all proportion, and from the top of the Capitoline Hill it crushes the whole of Rome as though you took the town in your hand and crumpled it up. It is dead-white too, and Rome is old living yellow and brown. They call this violated city the "third Rome"—characteristically ignoring the Middle Ages, but it is the fourth. Ancient Rome was destroyed by fire and sword, Medieval Rome by the pick-axe, Renaissance Rome—the most flagrant and triumphant of all—is being superseded by the jerry-builders. . . .

VIOLA MEYNELL Alice Meynell: A Memoir

All these Victorian writers were ardent strollers in Rome. This is how I see it.

## Italian Strolling

The stroll has always been a Roman pleasure, and as regards the possibility of indulging it there was no need for change from the time of the Scipios till about 1948 when the traffic first began to drive poor pedestrians to look for shelter. The stroll as a pleasure spread northwards from the Mediterranean and was one of the formative influences of the so-called "Latin" civilisation. It is one of the greatest pleasures that exist. But to enjoy it demands a whole interconnection of material conditions which are not expensive but part of the way of life of the Latin or "stroll" civilisation.

The "stroll" civilisation is perhaps originally an out-of-doors one, which demands a good climate. But this isn't absolutely necessary because even in Italy there are bouts of torrential rain or icy winds (the *tramontana*, or wind from the mountains). The stroll is not primarily a country affair: the solitary walker with his haversack on his back who climbs mountains is not a participant in the "stroll" civilisation. Strolling is a kind of social and aesthetic experience. It demands that both town and country should have some of the advantages of the other. Wild country doesn't appeal to the stroller as the pleasure it gives is not really aesthetic—it fills the heart with shaggy emotions of closeness to nature and religious feelings which are pantheistic and without clear and architected shapes. Moreover it involves effort and deprivations which interfere with the tranquillity and pleasure.

One can't stroll peaceably through thick grass or brambles which are always tripping one, or up and down steep hills that make one go at an uneven pace and get out of breath. Hence the hills must be improved by man's artifice and be flattened or used as decoration for the stroller's path beneath them. Tamed nature is made into gardens with paths and arbours. The trees are planted and clipped in regular order and, as they are of their nature monotonous, they are relieved by little arbours, temples, fountains of cool water and garden gods. Naked nymphs suggesting coolness and womanhood can be placed agreeably on the fountains, pouring out the water or preparing to bathe in it. All rich Romans have enjoyed their gardens, whether patricians of the old order or cardinals of the new. There is no reason to think that the gardens of Lucullus or Sallust in ancient Rome were any different in spirit or layout from, say, the Borghese gardens before they were opened to the public, or the gardens of the Villa Medici, the Villa Doria-Pamphili, the Quirinal or the Vatican today. Perhaps the most deservedly famous of these improvements on nature near Rome is the Villa d'Este at Tivoli with its symmetrical gardens, water engineering, fountains and cypresses.

The stroller also needs cover for wet and windy days, hence the development of colonnades, porticos and loggias. Rome, whether imperial or papal, has always been provided with these essential amenities. The stroll in the shelter of the colonnade or the portico, which was a social and aesthetic delight to the Latin poets, developed into the meditation in the cloister. Walking up and down at a slow pace, one's eye resting occasionally on the fountain in the centre of the cloister or on the architectures and statuary around and above, has at all times been a custom of priests and monks who have helped, of course, to mould and propagate the "stroll" civilisation. Rich Romans or cardinals could have colonnades and porticos of their own, but the poor have had to be satisfied with the architectures provided for the use of the public. There seem to have been more and better colonnades and other public strolling places for rainy days in ancient Rome than there are nowadays—today Bologna is the only city where the architecture has been made almost completely satisfactory in this way with its network of covered arcades. Even so Rome has a hint of a covered market in the glass-roofed Gallerie in the Piazza Colonna—and there are few more impressive strolling places in the world than Piazza Navona, the Campo dei Fiori, the Pincio and the piazzas round the great basilicas. In Italian cities these public places are, as it were, extensions of one's house, they belong to one as part of it. In some ways they are more important than one's house, at least as regards social life.

\* \* \* \* \* \*

The stroller needs another amenity which is always provided in the stroll civilisation and is another sign of it: a place where he can stop. Thus cafés and restaurants came into their own. The cafés of Italy are poor compared with those of France. There is about one table for over twenty clients, there is much pushing and pulling at the long chrome bar behind which the servers in white stand by their espresso machines and in front of their coloured shelves of aperitifs and liqueurs (cafés do not serve wine). A bar of this kind has even invaded the Caffè Greco, and Aragno in the Corso. The crowdedness, the ugly shininess and uprootedness of these bars seem inexplicable at first. They are little better than English tea-shops. Then one remembers once more that Italians can take their rest standing, they can talk for hours standing, they are in the direct line from Socrates who could philosophise on one leg like a stork, and—it brought home to one—from the Roman poets who stood chatting in a portico.

BERNARD WALL A City and a World

But getting about in Rome is a very different business nowadays.

## Getting About

From the Piazza Minerva to Trastevere is very little distance on foot, and I have walked it hundreds of times. One's legs are as strong at fifty as at thirty, only the inside of one's body curls up. But worse is the traffic. Down the

*Loreto: whole villages go on pilgrimage to the shrines of Italy*

*Rome: winter in the Borghese Gardens*

via del Gesù to the piazza is easy, but how to cross the Corso Vittorio? Along it the electric buses on rubber tyres hiss and sing. The singing comes from the trolleys against the wires. The hissing occurs when they stop and the driver presses the lever that opens the doors and lets the sardine passengers out. Behind them as they lumber along to the Largo Argentina—where there is the theatre and which is more or less on the site where Caesar was murdered—are streams of little Fiat cars, like beetles in a race. . . .

It is still possible to cross the Corso Vittorio to the protection of the dark wall of the Gesù if one waits for about five minutes. Meanwhile a crowd assembles. We all have the intention of crossing, and we feel like those desolate souls in Dante's Hell waiting to be ferried across the Styx. There is safety in numbers and even the ferocious drivers, knees up in their baby Fiats, are hesitant when they see our phalanx making ready to advance into the tide. "*Avanti*" says a cocky little man in the apron of a street sweeper, though himself not making a move. Our sub-consciousnesses are all in telepathic contact for at a given moment we move in unison. Only there is a jockeying for positions. The ideal situation for crossing a street is to be between two people, one on the right and one on the left, who would operate as bumpers against the metal surge; the drivers would slow down when they hit them and give one a chance to leap aside. The cocky little street sweeper did exactly this, but the bumper to our left was a girl with long blonde hair so the traffic slowed down automatically to look at her. Soon here, as in the Corso and other main streets, they will put up those lights which now and again flash a little green picture of a foot-slogger, telling one it is time to cross. Or else there will be underground passages as in Piazza Colonna, by the side of Constantine's column, or at the Largo Tritone.

I must brush aside thoughts of these little Piccadilly subways, with their glass and aluminium show windows, for they are depressing and opposed to "nature" and contemplation, like the traffic. The Romans love them, for in no city in the world is there a greater concentration of passion on "making things new." The Romans love all that is *novecento*, i.e. twentieth century and of the nuclear age. As I have said, in Parioli and the Quartieri Alti to the north of the city there are thousands of acres of ultra-modern concrete flats. All those streets from via Archimede to via Bruno Buozzi, then the whole area named after cities from viale Liegi to via Panama that stretch up to the park of Villa Savoia, then the area of streets named after rivers—via Reno, and via Tagliamento—and then those named after musicians—via Monteverdi, via Cimorosa, via Bellini—all have this characterless clean concrete in common. The flats are expensive, costing at least 100,000 lire a month, and have tubular steel and chromium furniture and silent lifts. That is where the bourgeoisie of Rome lives its Californian existence. The smallest of these flats have a tiny hole in the wall, windowless, beyond the shiny kitchen. In it there is a rough metal bed, a chair and on the wall a crucifix. That is where the servant lives. O the servants of Rome who aren't Romans at all, but wild creatures from the Abruzzi or Sardinia or—in higher demand—from Friuli or the Trentino near the blond Austrian border.

BERNARD WALL *A City and a World*

Roman churches are more than mere places of devotion. They are grandiose palace halls where one can meet and stroll about. The Gesù is the famous church of the Jesuits.

## *The Gesù*

On the 31st [1873] we went to the musical vesper-service at the Gesù—hitherto done so splendidly before the Pope and the cardinals. The manner of it was eloquent of change —no Pope, no cardinals, and indifferent music; but a great *mise en scène* nevertheless. The church is gorgeous; late Renaissance, of great proportions, and full, like so many others, but in a pre-eminent degree, of seventeenth- and eighteenth-century Romanism. It doesn't impress the imagination, but richly feeds the curiosity, by which I mean one's sense of the curious; suggests no legends, but innumerable anecdotes à la Stendhal. There is a vast dome, filled with a florid concave fresco of tumbling foreshortened angels, and all over the ceilings and cornices a wonderful outlay of dusky gildings and mouldings. There are various Bernini saints and seraphs in stucco-sculpture, astride of the tablets and door-tops, backing against their rusty machinery of coppery *nimbi* and egg-shaped cloudlets. Marble, damask and tapers in gorgeous profusion. The high altar a great screen of twinkling chandeliers. The choir perched in a little loft high up in the right transept, like a balcony in a side-scene at the opera, and indulging in surprising roulades and flourishes. . . . Near me sat a handsome, opulent-looking nun—possibly an abbess or prioress of noble lineage. Can a holy woman of such a complexion listen to a fine operatic baritone in a sumptuous temple and receive none but ascetic impressions? What a cross-fire of influences does Catholicism provide!

HENRY JAMES *Italian Hours*

Life in the Rome of the Popes was gay with festivals, of which the wildest was the Carnival—before Lent. But there were plenty of other holidays.

## *The Corso*

The Roman Carnival collects in the Corso. This street limits and determines the public celebration of these days. Anywhere else it would be a different sort of festival, and we have therefore first of all to describe the Corso.

Like several long streets of Italian towns, it derives its name from the horse-races which conclude the entertainment of each Carnival evening, and with which too, in other places, other festivals, such as that of the patron saint of the consecration of a church, are ended.

The street runs in a straight line from the Piazza del Popolo to the Piazza di Venezia; about three thousand five hundred paces long, and enclosed by high, mostly splendid buildings. Its breadth is not proportionate to its length, nor to the height of its edifices. The pavements for foot passengers take up on both sides from six to eight feet. The space in the middle for carriages is at most places from twelve to fourteen feet wide, and therefore, as will be readily calculated, allows but three vehicles at the most to drive abreast.

The obelisk on the Piazza del Popolo is, during the Carnival, the extreme limit of this street at the lower end, the Venetian Palace at the upper end.

On all Sundays and festival days of the year the Roman Corso is a scene of animation. The Romans of wealth and distinction take their drives here an hour or an hour and a half before nightfall in a long continuous line. The carriages start from the Venetian Palace, keeping the left side, and in fine weather they pass the obelisk, drive through the gate, on to the Flaminian way, sometimes as far as Ponte Molle.

On returning at an earlier or later hour, they keep the other side, so that the two lines of carriages pass each other in opposite directions in the best order.

Ambassadors have the right of driving up and down between the rows; this distinction was also allowed the Pretender, who stayed in Rome under the name of Duke of Albany.

The moment, however, the bells have sounded night this order is interrupted. Each one turns the way it pleases him, seeking his nearest road home, often to the inconvenience of many other equipages, which get impeded and stopped in the narrow space.

The evening drive, which is a brilliant affair in all great Italian towns, and is imitated in each small town, if only with a few coaches, attracts many foot passengers into the Corso; each one coming to see or to be seen.

The Carnival, as we may soon more particularly observe, is, in fact, but a continuation or rather the climax of the usual Sunday and festival-day recreations; it is nothing eccentric, nothing foreign, nothing unique, but attaches itself quite naturally to the general Roman style of living.

JOHANN WOLFGANG VON GOETHE *Travels in Italy*

It was not papal Rome—she of the Seven Hills—that attracted English visitors in the eighteenth and nineteenth centuries. Most of them tried to evoke from the ruins of ancient Rome the ghosts of poets and emperors.

## Rome Ruins

After a sleepless night, I trod, with a lofty step, the ruins of the Forum; each memorable spot where Romulus stood, or Tully spoke, or Caesar fell, was at once present to my eye; and several days of intoxication were lost or enjoyed before I could descend to a cool and minute investigation.

EDWARD GIBBON Autobiography

At one time it seemed almost obligatory to lament over Rome's lost glories. But whether the world gained or lost by the break-up of the Roman Empire is another question.

## City of the Soul

Oh Rome! my country! city of the soul!
The orphans of the heart must turn to thee,
Lone mother of dead empires! and control
In their shut breasts their petty misery.
What are our woes and sufferance? Come and see
The cypress, hear the owl, and plot your way
O'er steps of broken thrones and temples, Ye!
Whose agonies are evils of a day—
A world is at our feet as fragile as our clay.

The Niobe of nations! there she stands,
Childless and crownless, in her voiceless woe;
An empty urn within her wither'd hands,
Whose holy dust was scatter'd long ago;
The Scipios' tomb contains no ashes now;
The very sepulchres lie tenantless
Of their heroic dwellers: dost thou flow,
Old Tiber! through a marble wilderness?
Rise, with thy yellow waves, and mantle her distress.

The Goth, the Christian, Time, War, Flood and Fire,
Have dealt upon the seven-hill'd city's pride;
She saw her glories star by star expire,
And up the steep barbarian monarchs ride,
Where the car climb'd the Capitol; far and wide
Temple and tower went down, nor left a site:
Chaos of ruins! who shall trace the void,
O'er the dim fragments cast a lunar light,
And say, 'here was, or is,' where all is doubly night?

LORD BYRON *Childe Harold's Pilgrimage*


Here is a reconstruction of a Roman triumph by Samuel Rogers:


## *A Roman Triumph*

                Along the sacred way
Hither the triumph came, and, winding round
With acclamation, and the martial clang
Of instruments, and cars laden with spoil,
Stopped at the sacred stair that then appeared,
Then thro' the darkness broke, ample—star-bright,
As tho' it led to heaven. 'Twas night; but now
A thousand torches, turning night to day,
Blazed, and the victor, springing from his seat,
Went up, and, kneeling as in fervent prayer,
Entered the Capitol. But what are they
Who at the foot withdrawn, a mournful train
In fetters? And who, yet incredulous,
Now gazing wildly round, now on his sons,
On those so young, well pleased with all they see,
Staggers, alone, the last? They are the fallen,
Those who were spared to grace the chariot-wheels;
And where they parted, where the road divides,
The victor and the vanquished—there withdrew;
He to the festal board, and they to die.
   Well might the great, the mighty of the world,
They who were wont to fare deliciously
And war but for a kingdom more or less,

134

Shrink back, nor from their thrones endure to look,
To think that way! Well might they in their pomp
Humble themselves, and kneel and supplicate
To be delivered from a dream like this!

SAMUEL ROGERS Italy

The Baths of the ancient Romans, whose ruins are scattered through the old city, were what we should call Turkish baths. They were also clubs and sports palaces.

## *Roman Baths as Clubs*

Let us follow one of the elegant youths of Rome into one of the great thermae. He is welcomed at his entrance by the *ostiarius*, or porter, a tall majestic fellow with a sword at his side, and by the *capsarius*, or wardrobe-keeper, who takes charge of his wraps. Then follows a general salutation and kissing of friends, exchange of the last topics and scandals of the day, reading of the newspapers, or *acta diurna*. The visitor then selects the kind of bath which may suit his particular case—cold, tepid, warm, shower, or perspiration bath. The bath over, the real business begins, as, for example, taking a constitutional up and down the beautiful grounds, indulging in athletic sports or simple gymnastics to restore circulation, and to prepare himself for the delights of the table.

The luxurious meal finished, the gigantic club-house could supply him with every kind of amusement: libraries, concerts, literary entertainments, reading of the latest poems or novels, popular or Barnum-like shows, conversation with the noblest and most beautiful women. Very often a second bath was taken to prepare for the evening meal. All this could be done by three or four thousand persons at one and the same time, without confusion or delay, because of the great number of servants and slaves attached to the establishment.

LANCIANI Ancient Rome

Shelley loved to meditate and write in the ruins of the Baths of Caracalla. Operas are now performed there.

135

## In the Baths of Caracalla

These *Thermae* of Caracalla, which were one mile in circumference, and open at stated hours for the indiscriminate service of the senators and the people, contained above sixteen hundred seats of marble. The walls of the lofty apartments were covered with curious mosaics that imitated the art of the pencil in elegance of design and in the variety of their colours. The Egyptian granite was beautifully encrusted with the precious green marble of Numidia. The perpetual stream of hot water was poured into the capacious basins through so many wide mouths of bright and massy silver; and the meanest Roman could purchase, with a small copper coin, the daily enjoyment of a scene of pomp and luxury which might excite the envy of the kings of Asia. From these stately palaces issued forth a swarm of dirty and ragged plebeians, without shoes and without mantle; who loitered away whole days in the street or forum, to hear news and to hold disputes; who dissipated, in extravagant gaming, the miserable pittance of their wives and children; and spent the hours of the night in the indulgence of gross and vulgar sensuality.

EDWARD GIBBON *Autobiography*


Rome university is now the largest in Italy—but there are still to be found students like those Augustine had to contend with. He sounds unduly severe about them, but he had much to contend with in his own character.


## Dishonest Students

I began actively to set about the business of teaching literature and public speaking, which was the purpose for which I had come to Rome. At first I taught in my house, where I collected a number of pupils who had heard of me, and through them my reputation began to grow. But I now realised that there were difficulties in Rome with which I had not had to contend in Africa. True enough, I found

*The South: what will he do—migrate to a job in northern Italy? or stay and think?*

*Naples: land of poverty and vitality*

*The ancient gods and goddesses never died in southern Italy. They began resurrecting in the sixteenth century and now they are back*

*The Roman emperor Tiberius was the most famous of all residents
on the island of Capri. He haunts his island like the demon of midday*

that there was no rioting by young hooligans, but I was told that at any moment a number of students would plot together to avoid paying their master his fees and would transfer in a body to another. They were quite unscrupulous, and justice meant nothing to them compared with the love of money. There was hatred for them in my heart, and it was not unselfish hatred, for I suppose that I hated them more for what I should have to suffer from them than for the wrong they might do to any teacher. All the same, students like these are utterly dishonest. *They break their troth with you* by setting their hearts on fleeting temporal delusions and tainted money which defiles the hands that grasp it, and by clinging to a world which they can never hold. And all the while they turn their backs on you who are always present, calling them back and ready to pardon man's adulterous soul when it returns to you. For their warped and crooked minds I still hate students like these, but I love them too, hoping to teach them to mend their ways, so that they may learn to love their studies more than money and love you, their God, still more, for you are the Truth, the Source of good that does not fail, and the Peace of purest innocence. But in those days I was readier to dislike them for fear of the harm they might cause me than to hope that they would become good for your sake.

SAINT AUGUSTINE Confessions

Roman sculpture is really a continuation of the Greek, Alexandrian mood—but it made a decisive impression on the Italians of the Renaissance. There is a direct connection of feeling between these two periods separated by one thousand five hundred years. Byron is alluding to one of the better-known sculptures in Rome.

## *The Dying Gladiator*

I see before me the Gladiator lie:
He leans upon his hand—his manly brow
Consents to death, but conquers agony,
And his droop'd head sinks gradually low—

And through his side the last drops, ebbing slow
From the red gash, fall heavy, one by one,
Like the first of a thunder-shower; and now
The arena swims around him—he is gone,
Ere ceased the inhuman shout which hail'd the wretch who
    won.

LORD BYRON *Childe Harold's Pilgrimage*

Pièrre Teilhard de Chardin, evolutionist, palaeontologist, and priest—and to my mind the greatest Christian thinker of our time —seems to have been totally uninterested in Rome, either ancient or papal. For one who thought in terms of the countless millions of years stretching between the stuff of the cosmos to the ultimate destiny of man, these two or three thousand years must have seemed a small space indeed.

October 19, 1948.

   . . . As I am half-way now, I suppose, through my stay in Rome it is time to send you some impressions and news. I had a very simple journey, but I only just saw the descent from the Simplon to Lake Maggiore (very impressive) and the plain of the Po (almost aggressively fertile, but monotonous). Night overtook us before we went through Tuscany. Fortunately I was met at the station. Since I have been here I am surprised to find myself living as the Romans live, but superficially, and very superficially at that. The city has made no great impact on me; I have been living too long in another world. But I immediately fell in love with the light and the climate and (old memories of Aix and Egypt perhaps?) I feel curiously at home among the umbrella-pines and cypresses in this Mediterranean setting. I haven't yet, I'm afraid, visited any of the museums (I'm quite capable, I know, of skipping them all). On the other hand I go for a stroll every evening before sunset on the Pincio or the Janiculum (just near here) from which you can see the whole city offering the gilded façades of its countless churches to the last rays of the sun.

PIERRE TEILHARD DE CHARDIN *Letters*

## Roman Restaurants

Among the hundreds of restaurants in Rome, there is only room to mention a few of each type. If you are entertaining business friends on a generous expense account, there are the Orso down by the Tiber, a restored medieval inn where Montaigne once stayed, with a fashionable dance place above; the Capriccio in the Via Lombardia where the film-folk go; the Casina Valadier on the brow of the Pincian Gardens with the best view in Rome; Alfredo's opposite the Mausoleum of Augustus, which specialises in *fettucine al triplo burro*; or the Binlioteca near S. Andrea della Valle, so called because its walls are lined with over ten thousand bottles (all full) like books on the shelves of a library; a speciality of the place is a slightly sparkling white Frascati called Acqua di Trevi. All these are smart, fairly expensive and frequented by Americans and the "international set" generally, as is the Open Gate Club, just off the Via Bissolati.

People who are lucky enough to have both an expense account *and* a car often take their "visiting firemen" to the Palazzi Restaurant, just outside Rome on the Via Camillucia, formerly the luxurious love-nest which Mussolini built for Claretta Petacci (but their mirror-lined and mirror-ceilinged bedroom and the bathroom with the double bath for them both to romp in and splash each other are kept under lock and key, to the great disappointment of salacious visitors); or to the San Callisto, on the Old Appian Way just opposite the Basilica of S. Sebastiano, which is built over the catacombs of St Calixtus—the speciality of the restaurant is *pollo alla Nerone*, grilled chicken served with flaming bay-leaves drenched in brandy and invented in honour of the Duke of Edinburgh in 1951.

If you have a car but no expense account you can find dozens of agreeable and reasonably cheap places in which to eat out of doors in the summer, such as the Tor Carbone, on a turning to the right near the end of the Old Appian Way; the Sibilla and the Sirene overlooking what is left of the waterfalls at Tivoli; the many cool, vine-roofed *trattorie* round Frascati and Grottaferrata; and fish restaurants at Anzio.

A Roman restaurant with an old-world atmosphere of its own and excellent food is Ranieri's in the Via Mario dei Fiori just off the Piazza di Spagna, founded a century or so ago by Queen Victoria's chef, Giuseppe Ranieri, who was sent by her to the Emperor Maximilian in Mexico in the hope (as Ranieri's brochure charmingly says) "that the joys of good cooking might mitigate the worries and the bitterness which the government of his American realm caused to that unhappy monarch."

For an atmosphere riper by nearly a couple of thousand years there are the Ulpia in Trajan's Forum, whose downstairs room is built in an apse of the Ulpian Basilica; Da Pancrazio in the Piazza del Biscione, which occupied part of the *foyer* of Pompey's Theatre, where Julius Caesar was murdered (and not, as most people imagine, on the Capitol); and the Apuleius on the Aventine, whose décor reproduces the room of an ancient Roman house and where you can, if you want to, almost imagine yourself to be Senator P. Licentius Bibulus or Consul Q. Pepsicola Ridiculus.

Two of the most agreeable all-round restaurants in Rome are Passetto's in the Piazza Zanardelli and the Fagiano hidden behind the ancient pillars from the Etruscan city of Veii which line the west side of the Piazza Colonna, neither of them very cheap but with an extensive menu and generally well filled with both Italians and foreigners.

Meat in Rome is inclined to be tough, for they have a habit of eating it too soon after it is killed, but you can rely upon excellent meat at the Taverna Flavia in the Via Flavia and at the Fontanella opposite the Borghese Palace. The latter is a Florentine restaurant which specialises in game such as woodcock and snipe, and serves delicate wild boar in the autumn season. It is not expensive and the clientèle is upper-class Roman with very few foreigners as yet. For *pasta* there is the original Alfredo's in the Via della Scrofa, less expensive than Alfredo all' Augusteo, which likewise specialises in *fettuccine* with triple butter. The Tyrrhenian Sea is not pisciferous like the Adriatic, and one of the few good fish restaurants in Rome is Corsetti's in the Piazza S. Cosimato in Trastevere, which organises its own supplies direct from the coast; if you order its famous fish-soup, do not order anything else until you have come to an end of it; it is extremely good but so filling that I have never met anyone who has seen the bottom of his bowl.

Most of the typically Roman restaurants are to be found across the river in Trastevere. They range from the Cisterna, where the waiters are in fancy dress; through Romolo's, which is next door to the old house where Raphael's mistress-model, La Fornarina, used to live and where in summer you eat under the vines in the garden where she is said to have entertained him; Galeassi's and yet a third of the four Roman Alfredo's in the Piazza S. Maria in Trastevere, where the diners sit out in the square of a summer's evening and look at the floodlit mosaics on the ancient church; down to simple but good *trattorie* full of local colour such as Da Checco il Carrettiere, the Antica Pesa and La Garibaldina.

ARCHIBALD LYALL *Rome Sweet Rome*

This is a reliable guide—but the Fagiano in the Piazza Colonna has now closed.

## Roman Bars

In a "bar," often hyphenated with the word *pasticceria* (pastry shop) or *gelateria* (ice-cream shop), you can buy coffee, beer, a variety of spirits, liqueurs and soft drinks, very likely also ices and sweet cakes—but never wine. For wine you must seek a wineshop—*osteria, trattoria, bottiglieria, fiaschetteria,* or simply *vini.* (Theoretically the difference between a *trattoria* and an *osteria* is that you can get food in a *trattoria* whereas in an *osteria* you have to bring your own if you want to eat with your wine.) That means that a "bar" is not a place where the locals settle down to a couple of hours' sociable and inexpensive tippling but rather a place for short drinks and hurried rendezvous and nervous indigestion.

The main feature of a "bar" will be an enormous

chromium-plated *espresso* machine, bristling with handles and valves, to produce the coffee for which the Romans crave. The Romans drink very little alcohol, but the majority of them seem to be incurable caffeine addicts. Some are rumoured to drink anything up to forty *espressi* a day. A short black *espresso* coffee costs thirty-five lire, so that forty of them come to nearly a pound sterling if you reckon in the five-lire tip left on the bar each time for the *barista*—who, by the way, is a barman and not, as you might suppose, a counsel learned in the law.

Connoisseurs say that the best coffee is to be found in a *torrefazione,* which grinds its own coffee.

The national drug may be served up in other ways such as a *caffè latte*—coffee with milk; a *cappuccino* with rather less milk, so that it is the colour of a Capuchin's habit; a *caffè con panna* with a white foam of whipped cream on top—what the Viennese call *Schlagobers*; a *caffè macchiato,* an *espresso* with a drop of milk; a *caffè corretto* or *con lo schizzo,* with a drop of brandy, anisette or mistra; or a *granita di caffè con doppia panna,* cold with whipped cream on top and crushed ice below.

These bars-cum-ice-cream-parlours minister also to the other craving of the Roman palate, namely ices. These are of an infinite variety and you had better make your own experiments. The various kinds on sale are usually advertised outside by the makers on a poster with their names beside the illustration, so that you have only to pick the *gelato* of your choice and ask for it or point to it. There is no need to be frightened of buying ice-cream in a good Roman *gelateria* or *pasticceria.* They are as safe as Gunter's. A *cassata* is shaped like the quarter of a cone split vertically. Its core is an ice formed of different flavours of nut, fruit, vanilla or chocolate, encased in an integument of harder cream. A *tartufo* is a chocolate mount filled with ice-cream, flavoured with Marsala and peppered with nuts and crystallised fruits. Roman connoisseurs consider that some of the best ices, and certainly the best whipped cream, are to be had at Giolitti's in the Via Uffici del Vicario. When you pass through the Piazza del Popolo, sample a *semifreddo* di arancia, the delicious speciality of the Café Rosati, which is an orange scooped out and filled with cream and frozen orange pulp. A *gelato* is an ice-cream; if you want a water-ice, ask for a *granita*.

ARCHIBALD LYALL *Rome Sweet Rome*

The telephone is a tyrant in Rome, and until recently the post was slow and Romans became accustomed to rely on the former for nearly all their communications. The worst telephones are those in bars.

## *Telephoning*

Giorgio's ideas that evening were different. He had of course to make one or two telephone calls from the machine attached to the wall—a diabolical operation, but Romans don't mind it. First you have to obtain the *gettoni* from the cash-desk: these are nickel or leaden coins about the size of shillings with a groove down the middle. Then, because the telephone is cheap in Italy like railways, it is at least evens that the number will be engaged (if you are telephoning to a woman the odds are far greater because women curl up by the telephone on sofas or in bed and talk for hours—a half-hour's chat is almost a minimum). Finally, when you have obtained the number and pressed the button that releases the *gettone*, there comes the business of hearing. The noise in a café of shouting voices, moving cans, and hissing expresso machines is something from which Romans can absent themselves. Unlike me they don't need to press the receiver very hard to one ear with one hand and press the other ear with the other hand. They keep one hand free to gesticulate at the telephone and for the rest smile at it, make loving eyes at it, frown at it or snarl at it with perfect ease. Nor do they pay the faintest attention to the next person waiting to telephone (if another man) even when he nudges them and says "Excuse me but . . ." or puts his face up against the receiver so that he too is virtually joining in the conversation. I have even known

143

him, when he fails to get any response from the telephone-
user he is standing by, appeal to the person at the other
end of the wire: "Excuse me, signora, but I have a child
with influenza. . . . She has a temperature and I must
phone the doctor." "*Povera bambina,*" says the signora at
the other end, "how many degrees of temperature? I had
a daughter. . . ." Giorgio's telephone calls were not without
friction. I heard him saying "Have patience" to another
man who wanted to take his place, and then, in an even
angrier voice, "*li mortacci tua*". But he came back smiling.
We were to dine at the *taverna* where he usually ate. There
would also be his cousin. It was rather proletarian if it
didn't displease. But one ate well.

BERNARD WALL A City and a World

Foreign visitors may, if they wish, join with more sensitive
Italians in lamenting the destruction of natural beauty in Italy by
the vandals who are spreading the canker of jerry-building and
advertising. The Roman campagna is being ruined; if the process
continues another ten years, its characteristic beauty (in the spirit
of painters like Poussin and Claude) will have gone for ever. No
country needs legislation about town and country planning more
urgently than Italy.

## *The Roman Campagna*

To get on to the Appian Way you pass through the
Porta San Sebastiano, once called Porta Capena. According
to Cicero, as you emerge from this gate the first tombs you
see are those of Metellus, the Scipios and the Servilii. The
tomb of the Scipio family was discovered here and has
since then been transported to the Vatican. It is almost a
sacrilege to move ashes and altar ruins: imagination is
nearer to morality than is commonly thought, and must
not be outraged. The tombs that strike our view have been
given names haphazardly, without being able to be sure of
what they are supposed to be; but this very uncertainty
inspires an emotion that prevents us viewing any of these

*Amalfi was once a maritime republic and the Amalfitani are devoted to their shrine of St Andrew. Here he is outside his cathedral, with his cross and suitable "putti", or baby angels*

*Calabria: a poor woman's offering to the Madonna. The dollar bills come from men working in the United States*

monuments with indifference. In some of them peasants' houses have been installed; for the Romans consecrated a great deal of space and pretty large buildings to the funeral urns of their friends or their illustrious fellow-citizens. They did not have the arid principle of usefulness which brings fertility to a few extra odd square yards of land by afflicting with sterility the great domain of feeling and thought.

A short distance from the Appian Way one sees a temple raised by the Republic to Honour and Virtue; another to the God who made Hannibal retrace his steps; and the fountain of Egeria where Numa went to consult the godhead of good men—conscience probed in solitude. It appears that round these tombs only mere traces of the virtues still subsist. No monument of the ages of crime can be found near the places where these illustrious dead repose; they are surrounded by an honourable space in which the noblest memories can reign undisturbed.

There is something singular and remarkable about the appearance of the campagna round Rome; of course it is a desert for there are no trees or dwellings; but the earth is covered by natural plants that are ceaselessly renewed by the energy of the vegetation. These parasitic plants creep into the tombs, decorate the ruins and seem only there to honour the dead. It is as though nature in her pride has rejected all the works of man since the Cincinnati have ceased to guide the plough which furrowed her breast; she produces plants by chance through not allowing the living to make use of her wealth. These neglected plains must displease agriculturalists, administrators and all those who speculate on the land and would like to exploit it for man's needs; but dreamy souls, as concerned about death as life, derive pleasure from the contemplation of this Roman campagna on which modern times have left no trace; this land that cherishes its dead and covers them over lovingly with useless flowers, useless plants dragging over the soil and never rising high enough to separate themselves from the ashes they seem to caress.

MADAME DE STAËL Corinne

# The Vatican

THE VATICAN City in the heart of Rome is the tiniest independent state in the world—its area is about 500,000 square yards and it has only about one thousand inhabitants. But it is a genuine sovereign state, with its own little army of Noble Guards, Swiss Guards and Palatine Guards. Entering the piazza of St Peter's and looking across at the gigantic façade of the world's greatest basilica, or around at the great arms of Bernini's colonnade, or up to the right at the block of the Sacred Apostolic Palaces, one feels, whatever one's belief, that one is in a world power-centre. The Vatican ceremonial is the most stately on earth. This organisation—now two thousand years old, the only one with an unbroken history spanning two civilisations, old yet still going strong, stronger than in earlier centuries—is at the very roots of our history.

As there have been over two hundred and fifty Popes, it would be absurd to summarise papal history here.

The first St Peter's was built in the reign of the first Christian Emperor, Constantine. The present building was begun during the Renaissance. Bramante was one of the early architects.

## Bramante and St Peter's

This admirable artist was most enterprising. He proposed to restore and even to rearrange the Pope's palace. Hearing His Holiness speak of demolishing Saint Peter's to build it anew, Bramante made innumerable plans. Among these there was one that astonished everyone by its magnificence and beauty. It is indeed peerless in art and perfect judgment. Two towers flank the front of the building, as we see it in the medals struck by Caradosso. The Pope determined to undertake that stupendous building and had half of the old building torn down. He resolved that in art, invention, arrangement, and beauty, as well as size, magnificence, and splendour of decoration, Saint Peter's should surpass the buildings of republican Rome. With his usual promptitude, Bramante laid the foundations and before the death of the Pope he had raised the height to the cornice over the arches of the four piers. He completed the vaulting of this part and also finished the vaulting of the principal chapel and of another chapel called that of the king of France. For this chapel he invented the method of constructing vaulted ceilings by means of a strong framework of beams in which the decorations were carved and afterwards covered with castings in stucco. The cornice is most elegant and graceful. The capitals, formed of olive leaves, and all the external work, which is in the Doric order, show the boldness of Bramante's genius. We have clear proof that, had he had means to match his conceptions, Bramante would have performed work never before imagined.

But, after his death, the work was altered by each succeeding architect, and except for the piers that support the cupola, we may say that nothing of Bramante's original plan remains. Raphael began to make alterations as soon as he was appointed architect, along with Giuliano da Sangallo, after Julius II died. At last, Michelangelo, having set aside all the varying plans, has given the building a high degree of beauty. Michelangelo often remarked to me that he was carrying out the design and arrangements of Bramante and that Bramante should have sole credit. The original plan was of almost inconceivable vastness. If he had begun this stupendous edifice on a smaller scale, neither Sangallo nor the other masters, not even Michelangelo himself, would have been able to make it more imposing, though they proved themselves abundantly able to diminish the work.

VASARI *Lives of the Painters*

If the Renaissance Popes were not strikingly devout, they were magnificent, if at times tyrannical, patrons of the arts. Pope Julius II was a fiery soldier as well as patron—and Michelangelo suffered under his master.

## Michelangelo and Pope Julius II

When he arrived in Bologna, scarcely was his foot out of the stirrup before attendants hurried him to the Pope's presence. Michelangelo was accompanied by a bishop because Cardinal Soderini was ill. He knelt before the Pope, who merely glanced at him, saying angrily, "It seems that you would not come to us, but were waiting for us to come to you!" (He thus alluded to the fact that Bologna is nearer Florence than is Rome.) Michelangelo excused himself and admitted that he had acted in anger, but said that he could not bear to be ordered away. If he was wrong, he hoped the Pope would forgive him.

Now the bishop, in an effort to smooth things over, said that one should not expect artists to know anything outside their vocation, ignorant as they always were. This remark threw the Pope into a furious rage. He rushed at the bishop with a stick he happened to have in his hand, crying, "It is you who are the ignoramus, with your impertinences such as we would never think of uttering!" And he drove him out, the ushers hurrying the bishop along with blows. His rage thus spent upon the prelate, the Pope bestowed his benediction on Michelangelo. He then commissioned him to begin at once a bronze figure of himself, ten feet high. Of this figure we must say that the attitude was majestic and graceful, the draperies were rich and magnificent, and the countenance showed animation, force, resolution, and an imposing dignity. It was placed in a niche over the entrance of San Petronio in Bologna.

When the statue was almost finished in the clay, the Pope went to see it before he left Bologna. The Pope said he could not tell whether the figure was blessing or anathematising the people. Michelangelo replied that he was admonishing the Bolognese to behave discreetly, and asked if he should not put a book in the left hand. "Put a sword," said the Pope, "for of letters I know but little."

\* \* \* \* \* \*

For this work [the Sistine chapel] Michelangelo was paid three thousand crowns by the Pope. He may have spent twenty-five for colours. He worked under great personal inconvenience, constantly looking upward, so that he seriously injured his eyes. For months afterwards he could read a letter only when he held it above his head. I can vouch for the pain of this kind of labour. When I painted the ceiling of the palace of Duke Cosimo, I never could have finished the work without a special support for my head. As it is, I still feel the effects of it, and I wonder that Michelangelo endured it so well. But, as the work progressed, his zeal for his art increased daily, and he grudged no labour and was insensible to all fatigue.

Down the centre of the ceiling is the *History of the World,* from the Creation to the Deluge. The *Prophets* and the *Sibyls,* five on each side and one at each end, are painted on the corbels. The lunettes portray the genealogy of Christ. Michelangelo used no perspective, nor any one fixed point of sight, but was satisfied to paint each division with perfection of design. Truly this chapel has been, and is, the very light of our art. Everyone capable of judging stands amazed at the excellence of this work, at the grace and flexibility, the beautiful truth of proportion of the exquisite nude forms. These are varied in every way in expression and form. Some of the figures are seated, some are in motion, while others hold up festoons of oak leaves and acorns, the device of Pope Julius.

All the world hastened to behold this marvel and was overwhelmed, speechless with astonishment. The Pope rewarded Michelangelo with rich gifts and planned still greater works. Michelangelo sometimes remarked that he was aware that the pontiff really esteemed his abilities. When the Pope was sometimes rude and rough, he always soothed the injury by gifts and favours. Once, for example, Michelangelo asked leave to go to Florence for the festival of San Giovanni and begged also for some money for the journey. Pope Julius said, "Well! but when will this chapel be finished?" "When I can, Holy Father," said the artist. At that the Pope, who had a staff in his hand, struck

Michelangelo and exclaimed, "When I can—when I can! I'll make thee finish it, and quickly." But no sooner had Michelangelo returned to his house to prepare for the journey than the Pontiff's chamberlain brought five hundred crowns to pacify him. The chamberlain excused the Pope, declaring that these outbursts must be considered marks of His Holiness' favour. Michelangelo knew the Pope and was, after all, much attached to him. He laughed at what had happened, the more readily because things of this kind always turned out to his profit, and he saw that the Pope was anxious to keep him as a friend.

VASARI: *Lives of the Painters*

We must pause in the Sistine chapel. Michelangelo's Last Judgment on the far wall is veiled during papal conclaves. When it was first painted it was a riot of nakedness. Counter-Reformation Popes ordered successive draperies to be added to the figures.

## *The Last Judgment*

But unfortunately, though born and nurtured in a world where his feeling for the nude and his ideal of humanity could be appreciated, he passed most of his life in the midst of tragic disasters, and while yet in the fullness of his vigour, in the midst of his most creative years, he found himself alone, perhaps the greatest, but alas! also the last of the giants born so plentifully during the fifteenth century. He lived on in a world he could not but despise, in a world which really could no more employ him than it could understand him. He was not allowed, therefore, to busy himself where he felt most drawn by his genius, and, much against his own strongest impulses, he was obliged to expend his energy upon such subjects as the "Last Judgment." His later works all show signs of the altered conditions, first in an overflow into the figures he was creating of the scorn and bitterness he was feeling, then in the lack of harmony between his genius and what he was compelled to execute. His passion was the nude, his ideal power. But what outlet for such a passion, what expression for such an ideal could there be in subjects like the "Last Judgment," or the "Crucifixion of Peter"—subjects which the Christian world imperatively demanded should incarnate the fear of the humble and the self-sacrifice of the patient? Now humility and patience were feelings as unknown to Michelangelo as to Dante before him, or, for that matter, to any other of the world's creative geniuses at any time. Even had he felt them, he had no means of expressing them, for his nudes could convey a sense of power, not of weakness; of terror, not of dread; of despair, but not of submission. And terror the giant nudes of the "Last Judgment" do feel, but it is not terror of the Judge, who, being in no wise different from the others, in spite of his omnipotent gesture, seems to be *announcing* rather than *willing* what the bystanders, his fellows, could not *unwill*.

As the representation of the moment before the universe disappears in chaos—Gods huddling together for the *Götterdämmerung*—the "Last Judgment" is as grandly conceived as possible: but when the crash comes, none will survive it, not even God. Michelangelo therefore failed in his conception of the subject, and could not but fail. But where else in the whole world of art shall we receive such blasts of energy as from this giant's dream, or, if you will, nightmare? For kindred reasons the "Crucifixion of Peter" is a failure. Art can be only life-communicating and life-enhancing. If it treats of pain and death, these must always appear as manifestations and as results only of living resolutely and energetically. What chance is there, I ask, for this, artistically the only possible treatment, in the representation of a man crucified with his head downwards? Michelangelo could do nothing but make the bystanders, the executioners, all the more life-communicating, and therefore inevitably more sympathetic! No wonder he failed here! What a tragedy, by the way, that the one subject perfectly cut out for his genius, the one subject which required none but genuine artistic treatment, his "Bathers", executed forty years before these last works, has disappeared, leaving but scant traces! Yet even these suffice to enable the competent student to recognise that this composition must have been the greatest masterpiece in figure art of modern times.

BERNHARD BERENSON
*The Italian Painters of the Renaissance*

The Castel Sant' Angelo, or Castle of the Holy Angel, is the round brick fortress near St Peter's in Rome. Originally it was the tomb of the Emperor Hadrian, but in later turbulent ages the Popes used it as a place of refuge—it is still connected with the Vatican palaces by a brick causeway along which the Pope could pass. It is surmounted by a bronze angel which gives it its name.

When Benvenuto Cellini, the great Renaissance metal worker, went to Rome from Florence to seek his fortune, he took service with Pope Clement VII who was himself a Florentine and a member of the Medici family. Unfortunately Benvenuto's residence in Rome was not entirely peaceable. He was a quarrelsome, lecherous fellow who invariably got into trouble with the authorities—you can still see hundreds of men with exactly his features in the working-class quarters of Florence. His cheek was unlimited, he always thought he was in the right, and one can't help admiring him for his courage and never-failing optimism.

Soon after Benvenuto's arrival in Rome, Pope Clement was besieged, and Benvenuto accompanied him to the Castle. A whole series of exciting episodes followed in which Benvenuto was the hero and saved the day. But I must add a word of warning. He was a magnificent, congenital liar, and you can never believe a word of his Memoirs from which this extract is taken.

## In the Castel Sant' Angelo

Thus I went on looking after my guns, every day being marked by some notable feats of mine, so that I acquired boundless credit and favour in the eyes of the Pope. Never a day passed but I killed some of his besiegers. Once when the Pope was walking round the keep, he saw a Spanish colonel in the Prati, whom by certain signs he recognised; for the man had once been in his service. While he watched he talked about him. I, who was alone in the Angel, and knew nothing of what was going on, nevertheless saw a man occupied about the trenches. He had a little javelin in his hand, and his dress was all of rose colour. Be-thinking myself what I could do against him, I took one of the gerfalcons which I had there, a piece bigger and longer than a sacro, and very like a small culverin. First I emptied it, and then loaded it with a good quantity of fine powder mixed with coarse. Then I aimed well at the red man, rais-ing the muzzle tremendously, for he was far away, and guns of this sort cannot be expected to carry with precision at that range. When I fired, I aimed exactly at the red man's middle. He had slung his sword in front in arrogant Spanish fashion, and my ball hitting his blade, the man fell cut in two. The Pope, who was looking for nothing of the kind, was greatly pleased and astonished, for it seemed impossible to him a gun should have so long a range; nor could he understand how the man should have been cut in half. Sending for me, he asked me to explain. So I told him what ingenuity I had used; but as for cutting the man in two, it was a thing neither of us could get at the bottom of. Then, kneeling down, I begged him to remove from me the curse of this homicide and of others I had committed in that castle in the service of the Church. Whereupon the Pope, raising his hands, made the sign of the cross broadly over my face, gave me his blessing and his pardon for all the homicides I had committed, or ever should commit, in the service of the Church Apostolic. So I left him, and once on the tower again I went on firing without stop, and hardly ever was shot of mine in vain. My draw-ing, my fine studies, and my skill in music were all drowned in the roar of those guns; and were I to tell minutely all the fine things which I did in that infernally cruel business, I should strike the world with wonder.

BENVENUTO CELLINI *Memoirs*

If you stay long in Rome, you may pick up the habit of seeming outspoken and disrespectful about sacred things. Please remember that my next quotation was not written by me but by a Cardinal who afterwards became Pope.

## What is a Conclave?

Do you know what a Conclave is? It is a gathering of old men, less concerned about heaven than about earth, some of whom make themselves out to be iller and more gouty than they already are in the hope of arousing keener interest among their supporters. Many of their Eminences never despair of being elected, for it is the competitor nearest the tomb who causes least repugnance. In such cases rheumatism gives grounds for confidence; dropsy has its advocates—because ambition and death play the same cards. The coffin is a stepping-stone to the throne. And a pious candidate will bargain with his runner-up as to whether the duration of the new reign has an obligatory limit like a loan in commerce. As you know all too well, the shepherd of Ancona burned his crutches as soon as he had put on the tiara; and Leo X, who was elected at the age of thirty-eight, took great care not to recover from a mortal illness until the day after his coronation.

LORENZO GANGANELLI (later Pope Clement XIV)
Letter, April 16, 1769

Nearly everybody nowadays knows how a Pope is elected, and how the election is announced to the multitudes who wait outside St Peter's for the smoke from the Sistine chapel that announces the news. This was my experience at the time of the election of Pope John in 1958.

## On Electing a Pope

Yet you must see the point of view of the cardinals too. What is essential about this process of electing a new Pope? For Roman Catholic doctrine Rome, Michelangelo, Vatican museums, Swiss Guards, controversial Sistine smoke, are accretions that could be dispensed with. The essential point for them is to elect the 261st successor of a (not madly attractive) Jewish fisherman. Essential for their doctrine is that that Jew should have a successor until the end of the world, and in direct line. The cardinals could be crusty or avaricious old men. They could poison one another like Borgias. They could meet in the attic of a whore house in Haifa and have naked dancing girls on their knees. But they have to provide a successor to the original fisherman. They must lay their phoenix egg. Architecture, art and court etiquette has merely concreted round this essential fact as pearls in oysters.

Would they be prepared in an emergency to face the primitive squalor from which their religion came? On balance, yes, I think they would. Here lies their unbeatable strength. In my guess they thought that Cardinal Minds-zenty of Hungary, martyr in our eyes, made a *brutta figura*. His job was in Rome, he should have dressed up and walked out of the American Legation in Budapest and faced the wolves like a Roman senator. If a cardinal dies of exhaustion in the process of electing a Pope, he has just had it, and that's that.

On the Tuesday I had rendezvous at the smoke, morning and afternoon. It seemed to me the Black families were well represented in the piazza, with English-cut clothes (they often speak English almost without an accent), shooting sticks and portable stools. So walking up and down in the piazza before the crowds really assembled is like being in the foyer of the Scala of Milan in Stendhal's time, and I loved it. C. was being very Roman and positively snuffing for the smoke. He said, "You see, I know my smoke. Every real Roman of Rome knows his smoke, only there are very few of us left. Good smoke is just one short puff, almost invisible. Bad smoke goes on and on. It's like the difference between a Burmah cheroot and a proper cigar. Only the Piedmontese don't understand this. The real evil came to poor Italy from Garibaldi and Cavour. Another polite Roman whom we met, buttonholed me and said, "I love England, but nowadays it seems to be ruled by quite common people. How do you explain this?" C. said, "Of course in my grandfather's day the piazza was different. Everybody came in carriages and the country people from Frascati and all around came in carts so the carriages and carts were wedged in a solid block." "What a wonderful swearing there must have been after the blessing when they were disentangling," I said. "Have you read Peyrefitte?" asked C. penetratingly, "he is bloody funny. Of course if Cardinal Canali *is* ill . . ." and then we went back to the rosary of court gossip—Agagianian, the Architetto, the Nephews, Padre Rontondi, ex-Padre Tondi, Sister Pasqualina, the embalmment and the oculist.

Meanwhile out of the corner of our eyes we were watching the little funnel over the tiles of the Sistine roof where the smoke comes out. It was the afternoon and after the frustration of the morning I somehow felt it couldn't be good smoke yet awhile. A bright-eyed little man, followed by a teddy-boy selling *Sede Vacante* stamps (stamps printed during a papal interregnum) at a premium, was crying *Osservatore Romano*, the papal newspaper. So as to sell he shouted, "It is Papa Montini: they've sent for him from Milan; he is coming in a jet plane. Long live Papa Montini." "This about jet planes is all balls," said C. I felt sure he was right.

Then out of the Sistine funnel there came a wraith of smoke that could or could not have been from a half-dollar cigar. "It is white," some shouted. "It is black," others shouted. "It is white-black, *così*," said the *Osservatore* seller, "in one aspect it is black, in another aspect it is white. Long live Papa Montini." C. took my arm. "If there is more smoke it will be bad smoke," he said. "But if the jet plane hasn't arrived and the cardinals are in a rage," interrupted the little man, and then moved off. We waited. "It is good smoke," said C.

My second torture now started. Some minutes passed and I was looking at the *Osservatore Romano* and then at the iron grey façade, enormously ahead of us. Then a tiny light went on on the left of the main balcony. The crowd surged forward and I was swept into it. The cardinals had laid their sacred egg. I had lost C. and my other companions. Wedged against my backside were three nuns talking Schwyzer Dütsch, and another Zurich or Lucerne woman of military aspect and wearing a clerical ribboned hat. Behind them were two tiny Indian priests. Ahead there was a group of

156

American seminarians who always come off best in Roman *festas* being a head taller than anyone else, and though polite are as immovable and muscular as Bernini statues. Behind there was an antlike crowd as far as I could see. We were very near Caligula's obelisk in the centre of the piazza.

Then I got crowd sickness. I am terrified of the human multitude as some people are terrified of heights. I felt I couldn't breathe. If I fainted, which was certainly going to happen, how would I be got out of the centre of a quarter of a million people? It was the end. The ambulances for the sick were invisibly far like the television trucks and anyway were run by the Knights of Malta who. . . . My death was as mean as my life. I pushed myself more firmly than ever into the Swiss nuns because I had a hundred thousand lire in my back pocket and the boy selling *Sede Vacante* stamps was hovering. I held out my hands and held off the buttocks of a gigantic U.S. seminarian so as to have air. I tried to count sheep, review my past life and look at the tart on my right. I tried to think, if it was the end, how could men die better than facing fearful odds and could I appeal in my cockney speech to the seminarians to form a scrum round me and shout for Notre Dame while I said my dying Pater Noster. If only something would happen up on that balcony. "The cardinals have constipation," said the *Osservatore* man almost in my ear. "*Forza*", he shouted with his hands trumpeted round his mouth. At last unconnectedly the crowd began clapping and bawling to make the curtain come up.

With maddening slowness they opened the balcony windows and began laying out the tapestry. Would my thin wrists hold against such powerful buttocks? Then, or later, they began appearing, all of them, little red figures on the façade, at the windows, centre, left and right—a crowd of cardinals after supper in a painting. If I vomited at this moment? Then, bless him, one of the Indian priests piped up politely to one of the Americans, "Would you kindly lift me onto your shoulders, sir?" "Come on boys," said the American. The military woman with the Swiss nuns looked angry. "*Forza*", shouted the *Sede Vacante* boy who, by now, I was sure was a pickpocket and would probably be selling anything he got in the Tor di Nona that very evening.

The loud-speakers round the piazza began hiccuping and coughing. This was it. A private conversation between two cardinals on the balcony boomed round the piazza. "But where is it?" "Here, you talk into this microphone." "But I can't see the microphone. Is it functioning?" "But of course it's functioning, can't you hear it? *Funziona bene, benissimo.* Ebbene . . ."

The clerical throat-clearing, it was Cardinal Canali, was hollow over the piazza. "*Annuntio vobis gaudium magnum. . . .*"

BERNARD WALL A City and a World

When Pope John XXIII summoned his Oecumenical Council in 1962, many expected that, apart from the pageantry, it would be a dull affair—that the thousands of ecclesiastics from all over the world would be dressed up yes-men. Instead, a minor revolution developed within the Roman Catholic Church: the foreign prelates—French, Germans, Belgians, Dutch, and so on—showed they were determined to shake off the centralised system imposed on them by the traditionalist group of Italian Curia Cardinals, the high civil servants of the Vatican residing in Rome.

It is surprising to learn that there was a similar outspokenness at the First Vatican Council in 1870. Why, then, did the Curia Cardinals emerge victorious on that first occasion? One reason lay in the temperament of Pope Pius IX, who supported them. Another was that the first Vatican Council had to be suspended owing to the annexation of Papal Rome by the Italians. But also very important, as we can see, was that in those days travel was exceedingly uncomfortable for old Cardinals, and they could not stand the Roman climate. The Curia Cardinals thrived on it.

## A Row at the Council

And now, March 22, occurred the one real "scene" of the Council. Strossmayer was speaking (Mansi, 111 (51), 72):

"The Proem ascribes to Protestantism all the errors of the day—rationalism, pantheism, materialism, atheism; but

158

all these errors existed long before Protestantism. And there are among Protestants many grave men who are a great help to Catholics in opposing these errors, as in former times Leibnitz, in our day Guizot, whose refutation of Renan I would like to be in the hands of all." (Murmurs.) "I believe that there is in the midst of Protestantism a great crowd of men in Germany, England, and America, who love our Lord Jesus Christ and deserve to have applied to them those words of Augustine, 'They err indeed, but they err in good faith (murmurs): they are heretics, heretics; but no one holds them for heretics.' "

The President, Cardinal de Angelis: "I pray you, Rt. Rev. Father, to refrain from words that cause scandal to some Fathers." Strossmayer went on in the same sense with words not caught by the stenographers; but he was cut short by Cardinal Capalti, one of the Presidents, who said it was not a question of Protestants but of Protestantism, not of the persons but of the heresy; modern errors do arise from the principle of Protestantism, private judgement; therefore it is not against charity to say that these monsters of error are derived from Protestantism.

Strossmayer: "I thank your Eminence for this instruction; but your argument does not convince me that all these errors are to be attributed to Protestants. I believe that there exists in Protestantism not merely one or two, but a crowd of men who still love Jesus Christ." (Murmurs.)

Cardinal Capalti: "I beg that you stick to what the schema says. There is no mention in it of Protestants, but only of the sects condemned at Trent. Therefore it seems to me there is no offence given to Protestants. And so I beg you to desist from such speech, which I must frankly say offends the ears of very many bishops."

Strossmayer: "I finish. But I know that there are many living amidst Protestants, who with all their heart desire that there be not anything put into the schema that may be a check to divine grace working among them."

Capalti: "It seems to me, I must say, that your anim-adversions have no foundation in the schema, that could make Protestants put forward their hatred of the Catholic Church."

Strossmayer: "I finish; but against one observation of your Eminence I must say just one word. . . ."

Capalti tried to speak, but immediately, Fathers on all sides murmuring, Strossmayer said: "I attribute this to the deplorable conditions of this Council. . . ." An uproar of indignation made it almost impossible to hear what he said. He went on: "I make another observation, very short, but which I hold touches the essence of things, and so moved my conscience that I can by no means keep silence. In the recent Regulation it is laid down that questions are to be settled by a majority of votes. Against this some bishops have put in a statement, asking if the ancient rule of moral unanimity. . . ."

The speaker's words were made inaudible by the renewed and increased murmur of general indignation.

Capalti: "This does not belong to the present discussion." Vehement applause: the speaker tried to go on: most of the Fathers shouted him down; they almost raged (*obstrepunt, vix non fremunt*); many called on him to come down.

Strossmayer: "Your Eminence certainly should pardon me. I respect the rights of the Presidents. I certainly, if that former eternal and immutable rule of a morally unanimous consent. . . ."

The speaker's voice was drowned in the uproar of indignation. He said: "I protest against every inter-ruption, I. . . ."

Fathers rising called out: "We protest against you."

Strossmayer: "I protest against any interruption."

The First President rang his bell again and again.

The Fathers generally: "We wish him to come down; let him come down."

Strossmayer: "I protest against . . ." and he began to come down. The indignant Fathers left their seats, all murmuring different things. Some said, "These people

*Sardinia lay neglected for centuries until DDT drove away the malaria. It is now building up for tourists, and there are the mines*

*The cloister at Monreale near Palermo is the very
essence of Sicily, a combination of northern Gothic
and oriental tradition, luxuriant, tropical, phallic*

don't want the infallibility of the Pope; is this man infallible himself!"

Others: "He is Lucifer, anathema, anathema!" Others: "He is another Luther, let him be cast out!" And all cried out: "Come down, come down." But he kept on saying: "I protest, I protest," and came down.

DOM CUTHBERT BUTLER
*The Vatican Council, 1869-1870*

## Falling Ill at the Council

Tomorrow will be the feast of St Philip Neri, patron of Rome, and the Pope and all the world will be at the Chiesa Nuova; but we of the deputation on discipline shall be holding a session at the Palazzo Vacari, the residence of Cardinal Capalti, our President.

The weather is sweltering, and all the world is broiling. Bishop Turner [Salford] has got leave of absence on account of health and is going. Bishop Vaughan [Plymouth] is about petitioning the Judges of excuses on the same ground, as medical men say he ought not to work himself in the heat. Bishop Clifford has grown very thin, though I hear not of his going. I am better in health than I have been for years, and I suppose I must stand on to the end. The Pope refuses to give leaves of absence himself, saying he is found fault with for it. The Judges of excuses are very strict, yet half a dozen cases are put to the votes of the Council by them about once a week. And the benches are beginning to look thinner than they used to do, though I suppose we would still muster six hundred votes.

The same day. The great question is debated daily, and daily new names are put on the list, and that still for the question *in genere*. Then someone for the deputation gets up daily, and occupies a third or fourth of the time. Today Dr Manning got up for the deputation and occupied an hour and three-quarters, obviously anticipating Clifford, who was to speak also this morning. Then came the Bishop of Galway for an hour and a quarter. Then Clifford for an hour.

The controversy gets wide and wild and involved. But meanwhile there are more hopeful things behind the scenes. For a week past conferences have been going on between Orleans, Malines, Simor [Primate of Hungary], the Archbishop of Saragossa, the Bishop of Ratisbon, and other French bishops on the other side, tending to an accommodation. I spoke to Malines this morning, who assured me that a plan was almost matured for an accord, and he told me some of the details. I think they would do, if they can be carried out. And I understand they are approaching near to being brought forward.

The attendance at the Council thins, and with the prospect of a month longer on the question *in genere,* something must be done.

BISHOP ULLATHORNE<br>
Letter quoted in *The Vatican Council, 1869-1870* by<br>
DOM CUTHBERT BUTLER

We have come a long way since the days of Pope Leo X and Pope Julius II. Here is an extract from the testament of the saintly Pope John XXIII, who by his sincere and affectionate character, not to mention his wit, aroused the admiration of Moslems, Hindus and Communists as well as of his fellow Christians.

## Pope John's Will

On the point of presenting myself to the Lord, One and Three, who created me and redeemed me and wished to have me as His priest and bishop, who showered me with unending blessings, I entrust my poor soul to His mercy; I humbly beg His pardon for my sins and for my shortcomings. . . .

The sense of my littleness and nothingness has always kept me good company, keeping me humble and quiet and affording me the joy of devoting myself as best I could to the constant practice of obedience and charity for souls and to the interests of the Kingdom of Jesus, my Lord and my all. To Him be all glory; may my only reward be His mercy.

You are my all, my Lord. You know that I love You. For me this is enough.

I ask the forgiveness of those whom I may have offended unconsciously and of those to whom I may not have given edification. I feel that I have nothing to forgive anyone, for I recognise as brothers and benefactors all those who knew me or had any dealings with me—even should they have offended me, scorned me, not held me in esteem, as they would have done rightly, or may have caused me sorrow.

Born poor, but of honourable and humble people, I am particularly happy to die poor, having distributed all that came into my hands during the years of my priesthood and my episcopate—which in fact has been rather limited—according to the needs and circumstances of my simple and modest life for the service of the poor and to Holy Church which nurtured me. Appearances of comfortable circumstances often concealed hidden thorns of afflicting poverty and prevented me from always giving with the generosity which I have wished.

I thank God for this grace of poverty which I vowed in my youth, poverty of spirit as a priest of the Sacred Heart and real poverty which sustained me in never asking for anything, neither posts nor money nor favours, never, neither for myself nor my relatives nor my friends.

To my beloved family of the flesh, from whom I did not in fact receive any material wealth, I can leave only a very great and a very special blessing, with the exhortation that it preserve that fear of God which made it so dear and beloved to me. That family, though simple and modest without shame, is my only real title of nobility. I have always helped it in its most urgent needs, as a poor man to the poor, but without taking it out of its honourable and contented poverty. I pray and will always pray that it may prosper, happy as I am to see in the new and vigorous offspring the steadfastness and faithfulness to the religious traditions of our father which will always be its fortune. My most fervent wish is that no member of my family and relatives may ever lack the joy of the final eternal meeting.

. . . The kindness to this poor person from all those I met

163

on the way have made my life serene. I will remember on the threshold of death each and all those who have preceded me on the last journey, as well as those who will survive and follow me. May they pray for me. I will reciprocate their prayers from Purgatory or Paradise where I hope to be received, not through my merits, I repeat, but through the mercy of the Lord.

. . . I shall await and receive simply and gladly the arrival of Sister Death according to the circumstances with which the Lord pleases to send her to me.

*The following was added after John became Pope:*

First and foremost I ask, pardon of the Father of Mercy for my numberless sins, offences and negligences, as I have so often said and repeated in offering my daily sacrifice.

. . . I renew integrally and fervently my profession of Catholic, Apostolic and Roman faith. Among all the various forms and symbols with which the Faith expresses itself, I prefer the priestly and pontifical Creed of the Mass, the most vast and melodious elevation, as in union with the Universal Church of every Rite, of every century and of every region, from the *Credo in Deum, patrem omnipotentem* to the *Et vitam venturi saeculi.*

# Southwards

PRETTY WELL everyone knows that northern Italy and southern Italy are unalike, that the north is go-ahead and industrial, and
the south infertile and over-populated. It is tempting to say that
only an accident of history united them a hundred years ago.
But in that case it was an accident of history that united England
to Wales or the Southern States to the Northern ones, and so on.

The history of southern Italy would make a book by itself.
But I am unable to write that here.

## *Naples*

Six weeks were borrowed for my tour of Naples, the
most populous of cities, relative to its size, whose various
inhabitants seem to dwell on the confines of paradise and
hell-fire. . . . On my return, I fondly embraced, for the
last time, the miracles of Rome.

EDWARD GIBBON Autobiography

The administration of South Italy under the Bourbon Kings
was spectacular and squalid; it was a world of splendid palaces
and ant-heap slums. The monarchy had an alliance with the
*lazzaroni*—the casually employed round the great harbour—who
helped to put down opposition in times of stress. The other King
of Naples was (and still in some measure is) the patron, Saint
Januarius, whose blood is kept in a precious phial and liquefies
twice a year. The liquefaction is one of the great popular spectacles
of Naples. And it really happens.

The law in Naples was spasmodic under the Bourbons. We
find poor Keats languishing in quarantine in the loveliest seascape
on earth.

## Quarantine in Naples

October 24, 1820. Naples Harbour.

My dear Mrs Brawne. A few words will tell you what sort of passage we had, and what situation we are in, and few they must be on account of the Quarantine, our Letters being liable to be opened for the purpose of fumigation at the Health Office. We have to remain in the vessel ten days and are at present shut in a tier of ships. The sea air has been beneficial to me to about as great an extent as squally weather and bad accommodations and provision has done harm. So I am about as I was. Give my love to Fanny and tell her, if I were well there is enough in this Port of Naples to fill a quire of Paper—but it looks like a dream—every man who can row his boat and walk and talk seems a different being from myself. I do not feel in the world. . . .

JOHN KEATS

Neapolitans are no Puritans.

## *The Neapolitan Character*

It is easy to see that, in a general way, the inhabitants of the Parthenopean region have deviated less than ourselves from the standard of rightness as regards these tracts of primitive feeling, the reason being that they received Jewish ascetics upon a foundation of classical culture, as man; we, "as a little child" whose organism was susceptible like that of the Pacific islanders when catarrhs were introduced. They were never taught to disrespect the *encumbrance* of Oriental dreamers—the human body, that exquisite engine of delights; the antagonism of flesh and spirit, the most pernicious piece of crooked thinking which has ever oozed out of our poor deluded brain, has always been unintelligible to them. That is why they remain sober when the rest of us went crazy. There were no sour-faced Puritans in Naples, no witch-burnings, no inquisition—the Neapolitans never indulged in these fateful extravagances; they held that the promptings of nature were righteous and reasonable, and their priests, whatever they might profess to the contrary, still share this view and act accordingly; anti-asceticism is the key-note of their lives, and pruriency, off-spring of asceticism, conspicuous by its absence in young and old, in literature and society. More than ourselves, they have kept in view the ancient Hellenic ideal of Nemesis, of that true temperance which avoids troubling the equilibrium between man and his environment.

NORMAN DOUGLAS *Siren Land*

Vesuvius and his moods are almost as important to Naples as Saint Januarius.

## *Vesuvius Erupting and St Januarius*

William Hamilton was irresistibly drawn to Vesuvius. "It is impossible," he wrote, "to describe the glorious sight of a river of liquid fire, nor the effect of thousands of red-hot stones thrown up at least 200 yards high and rolling down the side of the mountain when they fell." After examining this eruption at close quarters he reported: "I thought proper to acquaint the Marquis Tanucci with what I had seen upon the mountain, and gave it as my opinion that His Sicilian Majesty would do well to remove from Portici. However (I believe on account of the smallpox being at Naples) the Court did not remove till two o'clock this morning when the explosions of the volcano shook the palace so much that His Sicilian Majesty was obliged to quit it hastily." The lava was flowing only a mile and half away. In the meantime the streets of Naples were full of processions. "On Tuesday the mob set fire to the Cardinal Archbishop's gate, His Eminence having refused to bring out the relics of Saint Januarius, and the same night the prisoners in the city jail, having wounded the jailer, attempted to escape but were prevented by the troops. On Thursday the mob was so increased and so tumultuous that His Sicilian Majesty thought proper to order the procession of Saint Januarius: it was attended by 20,000 people at least. . . . After having loaded their Saint with the grossest abuse for having suffered the mountain to give them these alarms, the riotous mob fell on their face and then returned to the Cathedral singing the praises of the Saint for the late miracle."

HAROLD ACTON The Bourbons of Naples

Sir William Hamilton, the husband of Nelson's Lady Hamilton, was British Ambassador to the Court of Naples during the French Revolution. He was a far more interesting and cultivated person than either Nelson or his wife—whatever the films say.

The Prime Minister of Naples at the same period was also an Englishman—Sir William Acton. The Queen of Naples was a sister of Marie Antoinette of France and was violently anti-French. Sir William Acton was a direct ancestor of the liberal Catholic historian, Lord Acton; Harold Acton is a collateral descendant.

## Nelson's Triumphal Entry into Naples

Nelson's spectacular entry into Naples on September 22 has often been described. What setting could surpass it for a hero's return from victory? People joyous by nature grabbed this opportunity for expressing their elation. More than five hundred boats and barges packed with singers and guitar-strummers rowed towards the *Vanguard*, badly battered by a recent squall. The British Anthem, "Rule Britannia" and "See the Conquering Hero" were repeated by various bands across the bay. The British ambassador's barge was the first to come alongside, greeted by a salvo of thirteen guns. Lady Hamilton, ever a mime in the grand manner, now enacted a scene which was to conquer the conquering hero. She had had three weeks to rehearse it. In a much-quoted letter to his wife, Nelson described the performance as terribly affecting: "Up flew her ladyship, and exclaiming, 'Oh God, is it possible?' she fell into my arm more dead than alive. Tears, however, soon set matters to rights. . . ."

To moderns, accustomed to a different school of acting,

the scene is hard to visualise without a smile. Lady Hamilton was considerably plumper than when Nelson had last met her, and she must have incurred the risk of knocking over the one-armed hero, who was short and spare, and not in the best of health. But "a fine figure of a woman" connoted *embonpoint*, and this full-blown, highly coloured rose expanding with patriotic fervour must have thrilled the simple-hearted sailor. An hour later the King himself climbed on board, saluted by twenty-one guns. His huge nose shone like a friendly beacon above his black velvet and gold lace, as he wrung Nelson's hand, calling him his deliverer and preserver. Among other compliments, he said he wished he could have served under Nelson at the battle of the Nile. The Queen was indisposed, having recently lost her youngest daughter, but the Princess Royal represented her though in an advanced state of pregnancy which caused her to swoon in the heat. With boyish curiosity the King wished to see everything, including the sick bay where a seaman was reading to a wounded mate, a sight which appealed to his sentiment, and the hat which Nelson had worn when his head was wounded. A lavish breakfast had been prepared for the guests. Even Commodore Caracciolo, most distinguished of Neapolitan sailors, came to congratulate Nelson, although he bore him a grudge. Miss Knight, who was of the party, recorded that a small white bird was also in attendance. She was told that it had alighted on the *Vanguard* the eve before the battle and had preferred to settle in the Admiral's quarters, though fed and petted by all.

From the moment Nelson stepped ashore he was fêted on a tremendous scale. Myriads of caged birds were released by fishermen, a symbol of rejoicing since time immemorial; and after dusk Nelson's name blazed from three thousand lamps on the British Embassy. "Between business and what is called pleasure," he observed, "I am not my own master for five minutes." Acton gave a sumptuous official banquet in his honour, after which the nine-year-old Prince Leopold presented a letter from the Queen, regretting that ill-health had prevented her from giving "Our Saviour" an audience. The

Queen had commissioned his portrait, and the little Prince said he would stand beneath it with the daily prayer: "Dear Nelson, teach me to become like you." The King felt he could not publicly entertain a British admiral while at peace with France, but he suspended Court mourning for the anniversary of Nelson's fortieth birthday on September 29. Every detail of this grand climax had been thought out by Lady Hamilton, from the buttons and ribbons with his initials distributed among the eighteen hundred guests to the rostral column, engraved with the names of his captains under the words *Veni, vidi, vici,* which was unveiled by the hostess with a Boadicean air. Miss Knight had composed an extra verse to the British Anthem in Nelson's praise. Wherever he moved he met with an ovation. When he visited the porcelain factory he was presented with the royal busts which he had intended to buy. But Lady Hamilton was worried by his meagre appetite. He was inwardly fretting to fight on against France.

At last the Queen gave him a private audience, and he could not help being impressed. "She is truly a daughter of Maria Theresa," he decided. "This country, by its system of procrastination, will ruin itself: the Queen sees it, and thinks as we do." Nelson, who never ceased railing at the French as "enemies of the human race," had met a feminine partisan. After his audience Nelson sat down and wrote a letter which was intended for the Queen, although it was addressed to Lady Hamilton, in whose house he was staying. This letter proves that he was not, as many have supposed, the innocent tool of a termagant in league with a Circe. After a review of the general situation he urged an immediate attack on France, ending with the words underlined: "*The boldest measures are the safest.*" These words were soon dinned into the King's ear by Sir William Hamilton, Acton, and the Queen.

HAROLD ACTON *The Bourbons of Naples*


I am no economist and should only waffle if I started "I think" writing about the economics of Southern Italy. When one is ill it is best to trust the doctor; when one's car goes wrong it is best to trust the mechanic; so here we had better trust the economist.

## *Southern Economics*

The regions comprising Southern Italy and the islands account for 38 per cent of the total population, whereas their contribution to the total number of births is 65 per cent. The Centre and the North, on the other hand, have 62 per cent of the population and 35 per cent of the births. This explains the apparent contradiction between the behaviour of total income and per capita income: in the South the former rose from 1,947,600m lire in 1951 to 3,266,600m in 1959, an increase of 67.7 per cent, whereas the latter rose from 110,000 lire to 172,000 lire, an increase of only 55.9 per cent.

In the same period the population of the South rose from 17,651,000 to 18,991,000, representing an increase of 7.6 per cent, whereas that of the Centre and the North expanded from 29,760,000 to 31,489,000, corresponding to a rise of 5.8 per cent. It should also be borne in mind that the increase would have been even greater in the South had it not been for the extensive migration of workers to more highly industrialised centres in other parts of Italy and abroad. This is another extremely important aspect of the progress of the Italian economy.

\* \* \* \* \* \*

Big industrial groups from the north—Montecatini, Edison, Snia Viscosa and Bombrini-Parodi-Delfino of Rome—have built or are building large installations in various parts of the South alongside the activities of the State concerns IRI and ENI. From 1958 to 1960 industrial employment in the South increased by 21.3 per cent, as against 13.6 per cent in the Centre and the North. During the next five years a decisive effort will certainly be made to bring the South of Italy up to economic and social levels more in keeping with the new European standards set by the Common Market. In this context the development of European co-operation, particularly in the form of greater freedom in the movement of capital and labour, is looked upon by national experts as an important factor for the future of the Italian South.

*The Financial Times,* January 16, 1961

What Boccaccio wrote about the south-western coast of Italy is still true. The tourist traffic does not get much further south than the Sorrento peninsula, save for a day's excursion to Paestum. The wild mountains and rocky coasts of Calabria are still empty and sometimes have a lunar loneliness.

## The Seacoast between Reggio and Gaeta: Ravello

Scarce any part of Italy is reputed so delectable as the seacoast between Reggio and Gaeta; and in particular the slope which overlooks the sea by Salerno, and which the dwellers there call the Slope of Amalfi, is studded with little towns, gardens and fountains, and peopled by men as wealthy and enterprising in mercantile affairs as are anywhere to be found; in one of which towns, to wit, Ravello, rich as its inhabitants are today, there was formerly a merchant, who surpassed them all in wealth, Landolfo Ruffolo by name, who yet, not content with his wealth, but desiring to double it, came nigh to lose it all and his own life to boot.

BOCCACCIO, *The Decameron*

The deep South, the toe and heel of Italy, only attract a special kind of traveller, one who meditates on ancient cities, whose sites we can still explore amid the dry rocks and the eucalyptus trees. Southern Italy and Sicily were the America of the ancient Greeks, their colonies there prospered and became independent, the cities became vast and luxurious.

Why did this civilisation disappear? Barbarian invasions? No, more, the poverty that has afflicted southern Italy derives from a complete change in the natural circumstances of life since ancient times. Greece has become barren in a similar way. There are no more trees, such as once held in the soil, the soil has been washed away leaving the bare rock. The goat, which nibbles the young shoots of growing trees, has been as much an enemy of this country as the Saracens.

## *Cotrone*

Next morning the wind still blew, but the rain was over; I could begin my rambles. Like the old town of Taranto, Cotrone occupies the site of the ancient acropolis, a little headland jutting into the sea; above, and in front of the town itself, stands the castle built by Charles V, with immense battlements looking over the harbour. From a road skirting the shore around the base of the fortress one views a wide bay, bounded to the north by the dark flanks of Sila (I was in sight of the Black Mountain once more), and southwards by a long low promontory, its level slowly declining to the far-off point where it ends amid the waves. On this Cape I fixed my eyes, straining them until it seemed to me that I distinguished something, a jutting speck against the sky, at its farthest point. Then I used my field-glass, and at once the doubtful speck became a clearly visible projection, much like a lighthouse. It is a Doric column, some five-and-twenty feet high; the one pillar that remains of the great temple of Hera, renowned through all the Hellenic world, and sacred still when the goddess had for centuries borne a Latin name. "Colonna" is the ordinary name of the Cape; but it is also known as *Capo di Naù* a name which preserves the Greek word *naos* (temple).

I planned for the morrow a visit to this spot, which is best reached by sea. Today great breakers were rolling upon the strand, and all the blue of the bay was dashed with white foam; another night would, I hoped, bring calm, and then the voyage! *Dis aliter visum.*

A little fleet of sailing vessels and coasting steamers had

taken refuge within the harbour, which is protected by a great mole. A good haven; the only one, indeed, between Taranto and Reggio, but it grieves one to remember that the mighty blocks built into the sea-barrier came from that fallen temple. We are told that as late as the sixteenth century the building remained all but perfect, with eight-and-forty pillars, rising there above the Ionian Sea; a guide to sailors, even as when Aeneas marked it on his storm-tossed galley.

※ ※ ※ ※ ※ ※

What has become of the ruins of Croton? This squalid little town of today has nothing left from antiquity. Yet a city bounded with a wall of twelve miles circumference is not easily swept from the face of the earth. Bishop Lucifer, wanting stones for his palace, had to go as far as the Cape Colonna; then, as now, no block of Croton remained. Nearly two hundred years before Christ the place was forsaken. Rome colonised it anew, and it recovered an obscure life as a place of embarkation for Greece, its houses occupying only the rock of the ancient citadel. Were there at that date any remnants of the great Greek city?—still great only two centuries before. Did all go to the building of Roman dwellings and temples and walls, which since have crumbled or been buried?

We are told that the river Aesarus flowed through the heart of the city at its prime. I looked over the plain, and yonder, towards the distant railway station, I descried a green track, the course of the all but stagnant and wholly pestilential stream, still called Esaro. Near its marshy mouth are wide orange orchards. Could one but see in vision the harbour, the streets, the vast encompassing wall! From the eminence where I stood, how many a friend and foe of Croton has looked down upon its shining ways, peopled with strength and beauty and wisdom! Here Pythagoras may have walked, glancing afar at the Lacinian sanctuary, then new built.

GEORGE GISSING *By the Ionian Sea*

Taranto has survived. Its natural advantages, as it is situated between a lake and the sea, have preserved it as a harbour—as it was in Roman times.

## *Tarentum*

There was a good view of Taranto across the water; the old town on its little island, compact of white houses, contrasting with the yellowish tints of the great new buildings which spread over the peninsula. With half-closed eyes, one could imagine the true Tarentum. Wavelets lapped upon the sand before me, their music the same as two thousand years ago. A goatherd came along, his flock straggling behind him; man and goats were as much of the old world as of the new. Far away, the boats of fishermen floated silently. I heard a rustle as an old fig tree hard by dropped its latest leaves. On the sea-bank of yellow crumbling earth lizards flashed about me in the sunshine. After a dull morning, the day had passed into golden serenity; a stillness as of eternal peace held earth and sky.

"Dearest of all to me is that nook of earth which yields not to Hymettus for its honey, nor for its olive to green Venafrum; where heaven grants a long springtime and warmth in winter, and in the sunny hollows Bacchus fosters a vintage noble as the Falernian —" The lines of Horace sang in my head; I thought, too, of the praise of Virgil, who, tradition has it, wrote his *Eclogues* hereabouts. Of course, the country has another aspect in spring and early summer: I saw it at a sad moment; but, all allowance made for seasons, it is still with wonder that one recalls the rapture of the poets. A change beyond conception must have come upon these shores of the Ionian Sea. The scent of rosemary seemed to be wafted across the ages from a vanished world.

GEORGE GISSING *By the Ionian Sea*

# Sicily

SICILIANS CALL Italy "the Continent" and their feeling of separateness is now recognised by their separate system of government. This is known as "regional autonomy" and is something like a mild form of Home Rule.

This is not the only thing that helps to make Sicily the Ireland of Italy. In area Sicily is far smaller than the Irish Republic, but it has rather more inhabitants—over four millions. Like the Irish, the Sicilians are emigrants. Nowadays they look for work in the industrial cities of northern Italy as Irishmen look for work in industrial cities in England. They are usually poorer than everybody else in everything save intelligence; they do not get on with northern Italians; and are rather looked down on in return. Big cities have Sicilian quarters which tend to be untidy.

Most of Sicily is a rough and hilly plateau, but there are high mountains in the north. Some of the mountains have oak and ilex, chestnut and holly trees on them—but others are completely bare. Where there is good soil the vegetation is riotous and luxuriant—date palms and India figs, agaves and prickly pears, pomegranates and vines. People fall on every inch of cultivable soil like ants.

The towns are often magnificent, if dilapidated—and their churches and palaces witness to all the foreign invasions the Sicilians have undergone: of Greeks, Carthaginians and Romans, and, more to our purpose, Saracens, Normans and Spaniards. Even a list of historic place-names seems evocative—Syracuse, Palermo, Catania, Messina, Agrigento, and Taormina, the tourist resort under the wing of volcanic Mount Etna.

## The Sicilian Character

Sicily in the middle of the last century was an incredibly poor, lost, backward country, Spaniards, Bourbons, one after the other they had killed the life in her. The Thousand and Garibaldi had not risen over the horizon, neither had the great emigration to America begun, nor the great return, with dollars and a newish outlook. The mass of the people were poorer even than the poor Irish of the same period, and save for climate, their conditions were worse. There were some great and wealthy landlords, dukes and barons still. But they lived in Naples, or in Palermo at the nearest. In the country, there were no roads at all for wheeled vehicles, consequently no carts, nothing but donkeys and pack-mules on the trails, or a sick person on a mule litter, or armed men on horseback, or men on donkeys. The life was medieval as in Russia. But whereas the Russia of 1850 is a vast flat country with a most picturesque life of nobles and serfs and soldiers, open and changeful, Sicily is a most beautiful country, but hilly, steep, shut-off, and abandoned, and the life is, or was, grimly unpicturesque in its dead monotony. The great nobles shunned the country, as in Ireland. And the people were sunk in bigotry, suspicion and gloom. The life of the villages and small towns was of an incredible spiteful meanness, as life always is when there is not enough change and fresh air; and the conditions were sordid, dirty, as they always are when the human spirits sink below a certain level. It is not in such places that one looks for passion and colour. The passion and colour in Verga's stories come in the villages near the east coast, where there is change since Ulysses sailed that way. Inland, in the isolation, the lid is on, and the intense watchful malice of neighbours is infinitely worse than any police system, infinitely more killing to the soul and the passionate body.

The picture is a bitter and depressing one, while ever we stay in the dense and smelly little streets. Verga wrote what he knew and felt. But when we pass from the habitations of sordid man, into the light and marvellous open country, then we feel at once the undying beauty of Sicily and the Greek world, a morning beauty, that has something miraculous in it, of purple anemones and cyclamens, and sumach and olive trees, and the place where Persephone came above-world, bringing back spring.

177

And we must remember that eight-tenths of the population of Sicily is maritime or agricultural, always has been, and therefore practically the whole day-life of the people passes in the open, in the splendour of the sun and the landscape, and the delicious, elemental aloneness of the old world. This is a great *unconscious* compensation. But what a compensation, after all!—even if you don't know you've got it; as even Verga doesn't quite. But he puts it in, all the same, and you can't read *Mastro Don Gesualdo* without feeling the marvellous glow and glamour like motes in a sunbeam. Out of doors, in a world like that, what is misery, after all! The great freshness keeps the men still fresh. It is the women in the dens of houses who deteriorate most.

And perhaps it is because the outside world is so lovely, that men in the Greek regions have never become introspective. They have not been driven to *that* form of compensation. With them, life pulses outwards, and the positive reality is outside. There is no turning inwards. So man becomes purely objective. And this is what makes the Greeks so difficult to understand: even Socrates. We don't understand him. We just translate him into another thing, our own thing. He is so peculiarly *objective* even in his attitude to the soul, that we could never get him if we didn't translate him into something else, and thus "make him our own."

And the glorious objectivity of the old Greek world still persists, old and blind now, among the southern Mediterranean peoples.

D. H. LAWRENCE

Introduction to *Mastro Don Gesualdo* by G. VERGA

### Sicilian Society

The most exact definition of the structure of Sicilian society would be that it constitutes a benevolent paedocracy: a society in which children hold the dominant power. They are the final cause of almost everything; towards them most actions tend; being most loved, they are most powerful. No single characteristic of the people is more striking than their affection for children. It extends to all classes, to both sexes and to people of every age. Nor is it merely a family affair: all children, no matter whose, receive fervent and immediate tenderness as an inalienable right. A wealthy and respectable man, should he see a woman in the street carrying a baby insufficiently wrapped, will at once, as a matter of course, go up to her and put matters right. If a baby starts to cry, it is the duty of everyone within sound to rally to amuse it. If strangers with a child enter a house, it is the child who receives the first welcome and attention. . . . Babies and children, even in comparatively poor homes, are well washed and dressed in neat, clean clothes, while their parents may be wearing patched and repatched rags.

\* \* \* \* \* \*

Children are wholeheartedly loved in and for themselves. They are loved for their innocence, their gaiety, their helplessness, but most of all for their pretty faces. In a country where life is soon worn out, where the period of flowering is pathetically short, youth and beauty are prized above all other goods. Women begin to lose their beauty at the age of twenty-two or three and by the time they are thirty, having given birth to perhaps seven children, are so occupied with their family that they have no time to care for their appearance. Thus children usurp the position of honour accorded to beauty, which in other countries is generally occupied by women. . . . The single room which constitutes the home is before all else a nursery, where the adults kneel in adoration.

The effect of all this attention on the children themselves is not noticeably bad. Since they are not nervous by nature, they develop without precocity or complexes, and since they have no toys, since limited space restricts their freedom, and because of the large families, there is no danger that they grow spoiled. The admiration they receive as children, however, is the cause of that supreme self-confidence which marks the Sicilians, a quality which often

179

tends to degenerate into self-complacency. This same admiration of children is perhaps also responsible for the great respect accorded to innocence and purity, the distinctive virtues of childhood, and for that satisfaction with a handsome appearance and new clothes felt by so many Sicilian men. As for the women, their inbred love of children is satisfied in child-bearing. In a country so prodigal of sunshine and where the standard of living is so low, the sacrifice involved in providing for a child is not very great, and is more than compensated for by the joy it brings the parents and relatives. If there are already older children in the family, these adopt the new child, again not out of duty but because they enjoy it. This co-operation is absolutely necessary in a country where it is not unusual for a mother to have to look after a family of as many as fourteen or fifteen. No sight is more characteristic or more engaging than that of a very small boy caring for his younger brother, amusing him when he is cross and teaching him first not to talk but to gesticulate.

The consequences of such large families are overpopulation within the island and widespread emigration, chiefly to South America, the United States and Australia. One member of a family will save sufficient money for his passage and, once arrived in the new country, will begin to put aside his earnings, so that within a few years he is able to bring his family from Sicily to join him. The effect of overcrowding on the island itself is that schools are swamped, educational progress hampered and primitive habits perpetuated. Shopkeepers even in the large towns can count only with difficulty and make mistakes in the simplest sums. Reading is a labour seldom indulged in, and when unavoidable is accomplished slowly, the words being articulated one by one. Not that the people are naturally dull or stupid: on the contrary, they are sharp and observant and in many ways clever, but it is altogether an outward cleverness, an astuteness of perception rather than an intellectual quality. It is part of their pattern of life, which treats existence, the mere fact of existence, as an end in itself. The physical enjoyment of life requires not great intelligence but quick sensations and to this end an alert response is stimulated by continual companionship and incessant talking. Only the shepherds in Sicily are ever alone: the rest of the population are always in company, usually parading the streets or, since the houses are inadequate, sitting at a *caffè*. It is a civic life, a life of talk and laughter which always takes place out of doors, and this fact is itself a reflection of the external and extrovert quality of the people. People in the streets, people continually passing, people talking and laughing and joking—this is the life of a Sicilian small town. In a country where comparatively little is actually achieved, where action is minimal, a flood of conversation acts to redress the balance. It is a play in which all the countless characters talk simultaneously and interminably, where the lighting is at full blaze against the most beautiful back-drop imaginable, and where nothing ever happens.

VINCENT CRONIN *The Golden Honeycomb*, 1954

All Italian religion is extrovert and unbrooding, but the further south we go the more the gods and goddesses of the Greco-Roman world emerge from their ancient shrines. There are far more miracles in Sicily than in northern Italy—only a few years ago when a statue of the Madonna in Syracuse wept, she received piled-up telegrams of supplication and sympathy. The Holy Family and the Saints are alike involved in the miraculous spirit of competition shown in the following.

### Sicilian Religion

Monday was the Feast of St Joseph. This was a minor occasion, for Sicilians, having more confidence in female saints than male, had reservations about Jesus. "Jesus was not much of a man," a fisherman told me. "A sort of feminine intellectual who never got ahead. He was inconsiderate of His mother, always making trouble for her, who was the greatest saint of all. His miracles were little ones compared to those of Catherine, Cecilia, and Lucia, who saved Catania from Etna. What did Jesus do? Chase some fish into a net and get Himself crucified because He wasn't man enough to prevent it!" A people with such an attitude about Jesus could not be expected to concern themselves much over the carpenter Joseph.

HERBERT KUBLY Easter in Sicily

Punch and Judy, of course, come to us from Italy. But the ancient and still popular legends of Sicily are about the struggle between the Christians and the Saracens—the heroic tales of Charlemagne and his paladins. Italian poets have written a whole cycle of semi-comic epics about the doings of those Christian heroes—Pulci, Boiardo and Ariosto. Ariosto's tales are a fairy palace of harmonies created with words. The Sicilian versions are rougher.

## Sicilian Theatre

I spent the afternoon in the town of Giarre, watching with an audience of children a Holy Week puppet performance. The *opera d'i pupi*, as the people call it, is the traditional theatre of Sicily. Until the invasion of cheap motion pictures, it was the most popular form of entertainment. Early in the century puppet theatres were as numerous as film houses in America. Today [1955] there are only four or five permanent companies operating in Palermo and half a dozen itinerant companies which travel to smaller cities and towns. The subject matter of Sicilian puppetry, like the heroic paintings on the donkey carts, deals almost entirely with the Saracen-Christian wars of Sicilian history. The plays, adapted more than a century ago from Ariosto's sixteenth-century classic, *Orlando Furioso*, and other historic accounts of the crusades, can run for as long as fourteen months without repeating themselves. I had visited one of these theatres near the Palermo waterfront. It was a dark, smelly, dimly lit room full of men and children. The performance went on for almost three hours, thirty acts from three to ten minutes long, jumping in action from Palestine to Paris to Sicily. At least once every quarter of an hour there was a noisy sabre-rattling duel. The Saracen villains were thick-skinned, jet black, heavily turbaned Negroid types; the knightly heroes were noble Norman blonds, always ready to sacrifice their lives for a woman's honour. The audience knew it all from memory. Throughout the performance men murmured to one another "Now will come Charlemagne," "Orlando will wait in the forest to meet the traitor Gano di Maconza." By listening to my neighbours, I knew two or three minutes ahead what was going to happen. When the evening's show was over, the puppeteer announced the coming attractions: "Will Ruggero overcome the traitor Gano and will he meet his love, Bradamente? Why is the beautiful queen of Persia disguised as a knight? Will Rinaldo recognise her? Come tomorrow night. . . ."

HERBERT KUBLY *Easter in Sicily*

The fame of the Mafia has spread far and wide, and Mafia methods have also spread—many of the famous gangsters in the United States were Sicilians by origin or descent who continued their inherited activities on more fruitful soil. The Mafia is a protection racket and behind it there are families rich and powerful in Sicilian society.

Yet nothing would be more unfair than to blame Sicilians for their traditions of violence and revenge, or for the lack of social order or equality in their island—especially from an armchair and from afar. Habits of violence are formed with centuries of misgovernment, when people decide to take the law into their own hands. The Mafia had confused and idealistic origins (we must think of it as something like the I.R.A.) which has continued and turned into a society for personal profit. The foreign invasions I mentioned earlier on should explain how this happened.

Danilo Dolci, the social reformer, has focused the attention of people in other countries on the miseries of poor Sicilians and this has helped to arouse concern amongst Italians themselves. It is from Italy that the real solution will come. Italy is now such a prosperous and going concern that, with time, it will be able to absorb the South Italians and Sicilians. I am not only thinking of government help which exists, but ever-increased employment and even the development of industries in the South. This change is happening all over the world; in spite of Home Rule the Sicilians, like the South Italians, are citizens of the same country as the Milanese, Turinese and Genoese, as the Scottish crofter is a citizen of the same country as the factory-worker at Coventry or Dagenham. But changes require time and patience, especially after a thousand years and more of troubled history.

## The Mafia

"Li Causi [a Sicilian Communist Member of Parliament] left Caltanisetta with ten others, among whom were three or four *Mafiosi*. Vizzini had already made his plans and he tipped off his associates at once, and when the meeting took place the square was full of men armed with bombs and pistols. Li Causi started the meeting by attacking the Mafia and when he said that both masters and workmen were being eaten alive by the Estate Managers, Vizzini said aloud: 'That's not true.' This was a signal to his men to open fire. In a moment, the square was full of smoke and people rushing about in all directions. A few minutes later, the only people left in the square were Calogero Vizzini and two others. All the doors were barricaded up and Li Causi, wounded in the knee, had taken refuge in a house with Pantaleone, who had fired his pistol into the air many times to frighten off the other side; they, in turn, had escaped to the headquarters of the Christian-Democrats and to other houses. Only one man on the Christian-Democrat side was hurt. Calogero Vizzini was a Christian-Democrat. The *carabinieri* sergeant never left the *carabinieri* barracks; there wasn't a single *carabiniere* on duty in the square, partly because they were too afraid and partly because they'd been told to keep out of the way.

"All over Sicily the Mafia exercises an intimidating influence on politics; if not in one way, in another. The Mafia wants to have its own way in everything. In the past it didn't take much interest in politics; but, today, it does in order to protect the interests of the large land-owners and so its own influence. They side with those in power and those in power protect them in their turn. 'So-and-so ought to go to America, or So-and-so is short of money,' they say; and the big-wigs pay up.

"The Mafia are all ignorant, uneducated fellows who've never been to school. Many of them can't even read or write. They have to call in their daughters or their sons to keep the fief accounts that they're supposed to be in charge of; whereas when a man's been in prison he learns things, because there I want to get on better than the next man and the next man wants to get on better than me. Everyone wants to do better than the next man in everything. Everyone has a mania for outdoing the next man.

". . . In the village we are nearly all illiterate, whereas, those of us who've been to prison have learnt many things. When I say 'Mantegazza this or Mantegazza that' [a celebrated nineteenth-century physician], they realise that I'm talking about important people and then they listen to what I have to say. You'd never guess how many things I know to impress people.

". . . When I went to bed, while others were saying their prayers I would say over to myself, before I went to sleep, what I had learnt by heart during the day, whether it was prose or poetry; so that, if there was a discussion going on, I could always give examples—'So-and-so says this,' or 'So-and-so-else says that'. So I was always sure of being right; for I was ashamed to admit what little schooling I'd had. When I'm in company, either at the Club or in a wine-cellar, I've a mania for explaining things. And people like listening to me; when I'm talking they're all as silent as the grave.

". . . On the 13th July this year, I was putting the charge in a mine when it exploded. I was blown into the air and lost part of my left hand; my right arm was broken; both my chest and face were pitted with bits of metal; and I was blinded in both eyes. Someone picked me up and took me to hospital, where I spent fifty days.

"When I went to the Pensions Office to ask for a pension, I was told I wasn't entitled to one. 'We've got you down here as a self-employed person,' they told me, 'and according to the law if you're a self-employed person you've got to be a "third party" at the time of the accident to get a disability pension. You weren't a "third party", and so you're not entitled to a pension.'

"What I've told you is perfectly true, although I haven't told you all I know. At first I answer with a knife; and, if I weren't blind, I'd be capable of answering with a gun.

"But I'm blind now and can't defend myself any more, or I could tell you many other things."

Quoted in *The Outlaws of Partinico* by DANILO DOLCI

# Postscript

THIS anthology is called a "personal" one. As such it has an excuse for being sketchy rather than systematic. Who in the world could cram into less than two hundred pages all that could be said about the innumerable cities and variegated regions of the country that has the oldest civilisation of a continuous kind in the West? Foreign tourists are now pouring into Italy every year not in thousands but in millions, and they have become an annual feature of the national life. There are few places in the summer months without their foreign visitors, sometimes in hordes, sometimes only a few. The wilder parts of Calabria and Apulia, or of Sardinia, still remain relatively unexplored even by that most adventurous kind of tourist, the young men and girl students with sleeping bags but no money who are now searching out into the most forgotten regions of the world. But southern Italy is rapidly developing and coming into contact with industrial civilisation, with the building of the great motor road south, and parts of Sardinia are joining in the race to attract tourists by building modern hotels and running air services to and fro from Genoa or Milan. The reader's first impression of Italy may not be historical or artistic. From his car window or from his motor bicycle he will see great autostradas round Milan and Turin with advertisements for international airways or the products of heavy industry. If he goes along the Genoese Riviera he will see a million or two people lying in the sun in summer on the rocks; he will see water-skiers wreathing in their acrobatics after roaring motor-boats; and if he looks upwards he will see jet planes and helicopters. The whole coast south of Venice in the direction of Byzantine Ravenna is one long beach divided up into bathing allotments called "bagni" and clustered with villas scarcely ten years old. Italy is now one of the great pleasure-grounds of the world, for those who take their pleasure gregariously.

But beneath the surface Italian life pulses on. Most of my extracts are of course taken from the past, but this past is after all the guide and key to why contemporary Italians are as they are. And most are from foreign writers, not from Italians. The possible quotations from Italian writers would of course be almost unending—but Italians know Italy so well that they take too much for granted. And I personally feel that the poets, Dante, Petrarch, Ariosto, Tasso and the others, hardly come across in English.

# Acknowledgments

Grateful acknowledgment is due to the following for permission to include copyright material in this book:

The Financial Times, G. A. Longo and G. Pella for passages from "Italy: a Financial Times Survey", 16 January 1961 (pages 13 and 171).

Jonathan Cape Ltd for a passage from *The Georgics of Virgil*, trans. C. Day Lewis (page 17).

Methuen & Co Ltd for a passage from *A Traveller in Rome* by H. V. Morton (page 18).

The Literary Executor of the Estate of Alice Meynell for the poem "The Watershed" by Alice Meynell (page 19) and a letter quoted in *Alice Meynell: A Memoir* by Viola Meynell (page 125).

William Heinemann Ltd for a passage from *Italian Art, Life and Landscape* by Bernard Wall (page 22).

Hamish Hamilton, London for passages from *Speaking the Language Like a Native*, © by Aubrey Menen 1962 (pages 24 and 117).

John Calder (Publishers) Ltd for passages from *Rome, Naples and Florence* by Stendhal, trans. R. N. Coe (pages 26, 53, 63, 65, 76, 107, 108 and 111).

Penguin Books Ltd for passages from *Confessions* by St Augustine, trans. R. S. Pine-Coffin (pages 29 and 136).

J. M. Dent & Sons Ltd for passages from *The Betrothed* by Alessandro Manzoni, trans. Archibald Colquhoun (pages 32 and 81).

The University of Chicago Press for a passage from *Mussolini* by Laura Fermi, © 1961 by The University of Chicago (page 35).

Gerald Duckworth & Co Ltd for a passage from *Winters of Content* by Sir Osbert Sitwell (page 40).

Faber & Faber Ltd for a passage from Canto III from *The Cantos of Ezra Pound* (page 43).

Penguin Books Ltd for passages from *The Quest for Corvo* by A. J. A. Symons (pages 44 and 47).

The Clarendon Press, Oxford for passages from *The Italian Painters of the Renaissance* by Bernhard Berenson (pages 50, 88 and 150).

Oxford University Press for passages from *The Castle of Fratta* by Ippolito Nievo, trans. L. F. Edwards (pages 51, 52 and 93).

Hutchinson & Co (Publishers) Ltd for a passage from *Pebbles from My Skull* by Stuart Hood (page 55).

Routledge & Kegan Paul Ltd for a passage from *The Life of Niccolò Machiavelli* by Roberto Ridolfi (page 58).

Edward Arnold (Publishers) Ltd for a passage from *Where Angels Fear to Tread* by E. M. Forster (page 59).

J. M. Dent & Sons Ltd for passages from *The Decameron* by Boccaccio, trans. J. M. Rigg (pages 60, 99 and 172).

Putnam & Co Ltd for passages from *Rome Sweet Rome* by Archibald Lyall (pages 62, 139 and 141).

Laurence Pollinger Ltd and the Estate of the late Mrs Frieda Lawrence for passages from *Etruscan Places* by D. H. Lawrence, published by William Heinemann Ltd (pages 72 and 73) and the essay "Flowery Tuscany" from *Phoenix* by D. H. Lawrence, published by William Heinemann Ltd (page 64).

The Bodley Head Ltd for a passage from *The Autobiography of Alice B. Toklas* by Gertrude Stein (page 77).

Chatto & Windus Ltd for passages from *The Charterhouse of Parma* by Stendhal, trans. C. K. Scott-Moncrieff (pages 91, 104 and 112).

Oxford University Press for passages from *The Literary Works of Machiavelli*, trans. and ed. J. R. Hale (pages 109 and 110).

Weidenfeld & Nicolson Ltd for passages from *A City and a World* by Bernard Wall (pages 126, 128, 143 and 154).

Stephen Spender for a passage from *Great Writings of Goethe,* edited by him and published by New American Library Ltd. as a Mentor Book (page 131).

Collins, Publishers for a passage from *Letters from a Traveller* by Pierre Teilhard de Chardin (page 138).

The National Catholic Welfare Conference, Washington, for an extract from their translation of the will of Pope John XXIII (page 162).

Martin Secker & Warburg Ltd for a passage from *Siren Land* by Norman Douglas (page 166).

Methuen & Co Ltd for passages from *The Bourbons of Naples* by Harold Acton (pages 167 and 168).

The Executors of the D. H. Lawrence Estate for a passage from the Introduction by D. H. Lawrence to *Mastro Don Gesualdo* by Giovanni Verga, published by Jonathan Cape Ltd (page 176).

Rupert Hart-Davis Ltd for a passage from *The Golden Honeycomb* by Vincent Cronin (page 178).

Victor Gollancz Ltd for passages from *Easter in Sicily* by Herbert Kubly (pages 181 and 182).

MacGibbon & Kee Ltd for a passage from *The Outlaws of Partinico* by Danilo Dolci (page 184).

Acknowledgement is also due to the following for permission to reproduce photographs:

Michele De Cristofaro (facing page 16); Bruno Stefani (facing pages 17, 33, 56, between 56 and 57 (Piazza Signoria), facing pages 57, 64. 81, 88, between 88 and 89 (Assisi), facing pages 96, 112, between 112 and 113 (Via Sacra), facing pages 128, 129, between 136 and 137 (2 photos), facing pages 137, 144, 160 and 161); Fiat (facing page 32); Fulvio Roiter (between 56 and 57 (Venice), facing pages 89, 113 and 136); Gianni Tortoli (facing pages 65, 80, between 88 and 89 (monastery at Camaldoli), and facing page 145); J. Allan Cash, FIBP, FRPS (facing page 97 and between 112 and 113 (the Trevi fountain).

The front endpaper photograph is by Fulvio Roiter; the back endpaper photograph of the Bologna-Florence section of the Autostrada del Sole is reproduced by courtesy of Firema S.p.A.